Pray the House Down

Kyle W. Bauer

Kyle W. Bauer

Copyright © 2019 Kyle W. Bauer
All rights reserved.
Unless otherwise noted, all Scripture quotations are taken from The Holy Bible New King James Version (NKJV), Copyright © 1982 Thomas Nelson, Inc.

ISBN: 978-0-578-61005-4

Dedicated to Pathway:
A church who is being readied by God
for the New Move of His Spirit

CONTENTS

	Introduction	7
1	Prophecy	10
2	A Season of Becoming	16
3	Prophecies for the Church	22
4	The Hands of the Potter	29
5	Waiting	35
6	Waiting and Expectation	38
7	Prayer that Brings the House Down	49
8	When The House Comes Down	60
9	The House Comes Down All Through History	68
10	The Works of the Lord	87
11	Pots of Oil	94
12	Personal Preparation	98
13	Service and Worship	109

INTRODUCTION

When we use the idiom "the house down" with any phrase, we know what is meant. This phrase has been in existence for at least as long as I can remember; when you "bring the house down" it simply means that whatever is going on is so intense, so stellar, so amazing, that the house cannot fully contain the awesomeness of what is happening. The mind-blowing greatness is too much for the house to handle—the house is coming down!

God has a House—and He figuratively and literally brought His House down. His House was the Tabernacle and later the Temple of the Old Testament. In fact, both Moses (the builder of the Tabernacle) and David (the planner of the Temple) said that God had given them very specific instructions to follow (Exodus 25:9; 1 Chronicles 28:19). The Tabernacle and the Temple were God literally bringing His House down from Heaven to Earth.

The Bible says that at the introduction of the Tabernacle, the cloud of God's glory was so intense that no one could enter. Later, at the dedication of the Temple, the worship became so intense and the same glory cloud was so weighty that the worshippers could not continue. God came down and filled the House He had brought down. The intercession, prayer, and worship literally "brought the House down."

Jesus taught us to pray, "Our Father who is in Heaven...let Your Kingdom come; let Your will be done on earth as it is in Heaven." Heaven is supposed to intersect earth, but it happens through a certain kind of praying: We are to literally "pray the House down"! But God does not dwell in a house made with human hands—He dwells in us; we are His House (1 Corinthians 3:17; 6:19).

But all too often, the "house" of our mentality, heart, understanding, and expectation is far too small to contain all that He wants to do in and through us. In order for God to bring His House down, He needs to do some renovation work in us to "build up our house" so He can "bring down His House." This is done in prayer.

I believe that God is gearing up to release, what I will call, a "New Move" of His Spirit across the earth. I believe it is an End Times move which will be the likes of nothing we have seen before. God's House is coming down to manifest, like in the Tabernacle and Temple, in fresh and powerful ways.

Get ready to *Pray The House Down*!

—Kyle W. Bauer

I
Prophecy

Every year I ask the Lord to give me a prophetic word for the new year. I do this because I believe God is always on the move and is moving us toward where He wants us to be spiritually in order for us to advance His Kingdom effectively through us asHis Church. We do not float on the winds and waves of life letting currents take us wherever they may flow we live with intentionality because God is an intentional God in everything He does. He knows the end from the beginning and He is actively working out His good purposes in this world. God created us to be participants along side Him, and He actively solicits us to take part in what He is doing on this earth. When we have ears to hear and a heart to obey, God will guide us in the necessary steps to take in order to grow and advance our lives and to be on the forefront of His plans and purposes.

Revelation 19:10 says the spirit of prophecy is the testimony of Jesus—Jesus Christ is the center of all prophecy. If this "spirit of prophecy" is witnessing about Jesus or anything Jesus desires to do in His Church, then everything about it revolves around Him; not any private interpretation or event happening apart from Him. Prophecy is commonly thought of as predicting the future, and biblically, many times prophecy has to do with the future. But prophecy is not necessarily predicting the future. Prophecy is revelation and understanding of what God is doing. It is hearing His voice, seeing His movements, and then proclaiming them to the people so we may be fully prepared to participate with what God is doing. Prophecy is lining up our actions and words with the actions and words of God.

Prophecy is different than simply repeating what the Bible says, though prophecy never will contradict God's revealed Word. Prophecy may come from a Bible passage with direct revelation by the Holy Spirit—this is not a "new" revelation that is contradictory to the Bible, rather an instruction, vision, or guiding word for a moment or season in which God wants to work. In short, prophecy prepares us for what is to come.

ACTIONS AND WORDS

There are both prophetic *actions* and prophetic *words* in which God reveals to His people the times and the seasons of His working.

Prophetic actions are demonstrated. Simply put, these actions are things we do in the physical that both represent and release spiritual realities into our present circumstance. The laying on of hands, anointing with oil, baptism, and communion are examples of representative physical acts which release a spiritual dynamic from Heaven.

Prophetic acts directed by the Holy Spirit are powerful signs that move God's people forward into His purposes. If these actions are not directed by the Holy Spirit, they are powerless displays of religiosity. Take the two examples of Zedekaiah and Joshua, for instance.

In 1 Kings 22 we read of the reigns of Ahab (in the North of Israel) and of Jehoshaphat (in Southern Israel), they decided to go to war together. Before they entered into battle, they consulted the prophets to see in the Lord was with them and whether or not they would have victory. Two prophets in particular stood up, one was Zedekiah who made horns of iron and demonstrated a prophetic act with the horns saying, "Thus says the LORD, 'With these you shall push the Syrians until they are destroyed.'" Then the prophet Micaiah stood up and delivered an accurate prophetic word from God which declared defeat in battle. Micaiah's word was proven right, and Ahab died in battle. The prophet Zedekiah did a prophetic action which was not directed by God. It was a fruitless action which ended up deceiving both kings into going to battle and leading them to defeat.

In contrast, there is Joshua, the second leader of Israel. When the Israelites possessed the Promised Land, their first battle was against Jericho, and they were given the most unusual plan to take the city: Be silent and walk around the walls many times for a week. Yet they were given orders by God to give a great shout at the end of the last lap around the city. They shouted and the walls fell down. Neither walking around a city nor a simple human shout are enough to break a thick wall—but they did the action at the direction of the Holy Spirit and it released wall-breaking power!

Prophetic words declare what God is doing. There are two Greek words in the New Testament that describe the "Word" of God. The first is "logos" which designates the written Scriptures. The second is "rhema" which is God's word given to speak into a precise moment or situation. Logos is written; rhema is revealed. Rhema will never go against the written Word of God. Rhema is a specific word revealed by God through His servants in order to align and conform a person or a people to His will. Many times a rhema comes directly from the Logos! In other words, it is a "word" of prophecy which is revealed from the Word of Scripture to speak directly to a situation.

Prophecy prepares us for what God is about to do. For example, suppose my wife prepared a wonderful dinner while the kids were playing outside. Then one of the kids comes in to the kitchen and my wife tells him, "Go and tell your siblings that dinner is ready." Then my son would go to his brothers and sister and would be the mouth piece of his mother, recognizing that his mother is one of the greatest authorities in the house and whose word must be obeyed. So my son goes and announces to his siblings, "Mom says to come because dinner is ready! Come on! Let's go eat!" This is, in essence, what prophecy is. It is not something invented, but it's something that God, who is the ultimate authority, is actually doing and saying. God makes the prophet understand what He is about to do so the prophet may go and tell the people. In essence, God sends His prophets so His people will be ready to participate with what He is getting ready to do.

The purpose of this short book is prophetic. I am

announcing to you what God desires to do. I beg you to have ears to hear and hearts to obey what God is saying to His people in this season in preparation for what is about to come.

2
A SEASON OF BECOMING

Our seasons of waiting and expectation are seasons of becoming. We are being renewed day-by-day, ever being changed in the glorious image of the Son of God: We are becoming more like Him, and when we are more like Him, we will be able to fully participate with the new thing He wants to release on the earth. Jesus addresses the issue of renewal and becoming more in Mark 2:18-22:

"The disciples of John and of the Pharisees were fasting. Then they came and said to Him, 'Why do the disciples of John and of the Pharisees fast, but Your disciples do not fast?'

And Jesus said to them, 'Can the friends of the bridegroom fast while the bridegroom is with them? As long as they have the bridegroom with them they cannot fast. But the days will come when the bridegroom will be taken away from them, and then they will fast in those days. No one sews a piece of unshrunk cloth on an old garment; or else the new piece pulls away from the old, and the tear is made worse. And no one puts new wine into old wineskins; or else the new wine bursts the wineskins, the wine is spilled, and the wineskins are ruined. But new wine must be put into new wineskins.'"

The same question was posed to Jesus that has been asked millions of times throughout Christian history in many different ways in just about every context imaginable:

- Why don't you do the same religious things we do?

- Why don't you fall in line with everything that is the traditional norm?

- Why don't you do things the way they have always been done?

- Why don't you see things the same way I see them in my air-tight theology?

Along with these questions generally come the attitude of "it is different, therefore it must not be of God." Whether it is restructuring the usher team, the Sunday morning service, the church décor, or a new vision for the church, we tend to have a hard time embracing the new. But perhaps the new thing God is doing is bigger than the theological or churchy boxes we have created for Him. Can we make room in our hearts and minds for God to be just a little bit bigger than us and our finite understanding? This is one of the things I love about God—He is so big and there is always more of Him to grow in and understand! Yet it seems that when He desires to grow His Church, His works are not always welcomed among His people. Sometimes they are denounced as heretical, fanatical, weird, anti-biblical, and many such other things. When there is no basis for these works in the Scriptures, then one needs to steer clear. But if there is legitimate Biblical understanding and basis behind God's unfolding works, then one needs to make a decision: Will I welcome the works of Jesus that take me out of my comfort zone or not?

Jesus responded in a sort of cryptic way with three very short parables, each taking no more than two sentences; a bridegroom, a patch, and a wineskin.

John's disciples must have been scratching their heads thinking, "What on earth do any of these things have to do with fasting?" Jesus didn't answer their direct question about fasting, because at the core, the question didn't have to do with fasting—it had to do with the works of Jesus and His followers.

The question was: Why don't you do what we do?

Jesus' answer was: Why can't you see what I am doing now?

Jesus said those who become disciples of the Kingdom of Heaven are like a house owner who brings out treasures "old and new" (Matthew 13:52). The old treasures are beautiful, but there are new treasures as well that are available to us. None of these short parables have to do with "newer is better," but rather they are moving into something BIGGER.

When I was single, I was responsible only to myself. I could go where I pleased and do what I wanted at the drop of a hat. However, when I became a husband, that small-minded way of living was no longer compatible with the responsibility of a wife and a home—and much less when children came along! My life got much bigger, and my way of thinking, doing, and being needed to grow along with the newness of life. As I Corinthians 13:11 instructs, "When I was a child, I spoke as a child, I understood as a child, I thought as a child; but when I became a man, I put away childish things."

The new patch cannot be put on an old garment—they are not compatible. There is a process of being made to fit each other so nothing is torn. What God did yesterday was a wonderful thing, but it is only part of the story, not the culmination of it. He is adding to and enlarging His story, and what was done in the past is the foundation of how God wants to build His Kingdom now. We must be careful not to "tear" the continued work of the Lord by living in yester-year and not receiving the newness of today.

The wineskin was a leather bag in which new wine was put to undergo the fermentation process. During this process, the gasses released would bloat the bag and harden the leather. Therefore, if new wine was put into a bloated, hardened leather bag, during the fermentation process, the bag would not be either big enough nor pliable enough and would split and both the wine and the bag would be lost.

Jesus makes a wonderful statement that can easily be lost on us, He intends that "both are preserved." There is a continuing work of God going on which is being built on the previous works. Preserve and treasure what is already learned, but be flexible enough to receive the new.

In order for the bag to be able to receive the new wine (which is a Biblical metaphor for blessing, abundance, life, and joy), it must be renewed. The process of renewal was to rub the hardened and crusty leather with oil until it became pliable again. Oil is a biblical metaphor for the work of the Holy Spirit. Every person—every church—every disciple of Jesus needs the constant, fresh, renewing work of the Holy Spirit in us to keep us pliable and in step with what Jesus is doing.

The religious practices of yesterday, though the cutting edge of what God was doing then, don't cut it for today. As with Jesus and His disciples, the issue isn't if *they* do things the way *we* do them, it is if we can see, receive, and participate with what Jesus is doing right now and right in front of us.

3
PROPHECIES FOR THE CHURCH

Over the past few years, the Lord has given me a few different prophetic words and visions which I have either kept to myself to pray about them, or have shared largely only with the congregation I serve. I feel compelled to share these with as large an audience as the Lord will give me, as these words are to stimulate us to pray the house down in preparation for what God is getting ready to unleash!

THE NEW MOVE
Early in 2019, as I waited upon the Lord in prayer and seeking, the Lord showed me a picture of a meeting in Heaven where several people were around a beautiful table in a beautiful, heavenly setting. I heard the leader of the meeting say, "God is getting ready to unleash a New Move!"

I heard some other things that do not bear repeating here, but there are two others things that we do need to hear: The first is that God is preparing churches specifically to help usher in this New Move, and secondly, there is intercession in Heaven going on for the Church!

I was moved beyond words. I knew I wanted my church to be ready for the New Move of God—and I want your church to be ready, too! If God is preparing to unleash something amazing on the earth, then we need to align ourselves to participate with Him to the maximum.

The Lightning Rod

God is doing something new, fresh, and powerful at our church Pathway, but it is not exclusively for us: I believe it is available to anyone who would avail themselves of it. At the very beginning of our pastorate at Pathway, God gave me a prophetic vision that will continue to guide us into the future. In the vision I saw an immense storm with thick, dark clouds and thunder and lightning. Then I saw the little A-frame building of our church sanctuary and from the roof a lightning rod stood up and was repeatedly struck by the lightning and the lightning rod conducted the electricity and released it on the Earth.

Shortly before the Lord showed me this vision, I

was wondering if the name "Pathway" was what our name was to be going forward. After this vision, I looked up the definition of a lightning rod and it simply states that a lightning rod catches lightning and moves it to the earth via "a conductive pathway!" It was clear to me: God is asking that the Church be a "Pathway" which catches what is going on in the Heavens and releases it on the earth in preparation for what God is about to do on this earth!

The Circuit Breaker

It was not long after this vision, we needed some upgrades in our electrical systems at the church. Upon inspecting our system, the electrician commented that our wires were capable of a very large load, but the breakers needed to be updated from 60 amps to 80 amps to let more energy flow through it without the breaker tripping.

What a metaphor for the Church! We, as God's children, are capable of capturing and flowing in God's supernatural power, but our circuit breakers are too small. In order for *all* of what God desires to do in and through us be released, He needs to upgrade our breakers! He needs to enlarge us. He needs to up our capacity.

For far too long, too many people in the Church begin to see something of God's power begin to move and their breakers "flip off" because we have been too small in our thinking, our theology, our understanding of God, or our understanding of His Word. When the breaker flips off (or with some people they "flip out" when things beyond their experience begin to happen), the electrical current is cut off and no more power flows. What a tragedy when God desires to do more in our lives and churches and our own smallness of understanding, or our unwillingness to let go of sin, shuts off His power—the breaker is tripped! God wants to do increasingly greater things in and through His Church; He wants to take us "from glory to glory." But this requires an upgrade in our relationship with Him and our capacity to know Him. I believe God wants to install a much larger circuit breaker in His Church. Perhaps the ultimate goal is to have none at all so there is never a limit on the amount of power God can flow into and through His Church.

A LARGER VESSEL

In 2016 the Lord gave me a prophetic word for our church. Since 2016, much has changed in mine and Teresa's lives and ministry, but as time has passed, I recognize this word is more than for only that moment of time in the church in which we were serving, but it is something the Lord would say to His whole Church; the word continues to be viable and active today.

It was during a Wednesday night worship service that the Lord gave me a vision. It was of a clay pot. Into the pot God was pouring a beautiful golden liquid of His glory and His anointing. The pot was very small, and it quickly filled up, yet the golden liquid continued to be poured out. It began to overflow out of the pot and run everywhere. The anointing was released, but this was not an overflow of anointing, it was wasted anointing because the vessel was unable to contain the full level of what God was pouring out.

I then saw the hands of the Lord take the pot and put it on the potters wheel. His hands went inside the lip of the pot, and as He spun it around, He began to form the pot into a much larger vessel. Once He had finished, He again poured out the golden liquid. But this time, the pot was able to hold what God had poured out and it was not wasted and lost. ***God wants to make us into a larger vessel in order to be able to handle what He wants to pour out on this earth.***

I believe God is getting ready to pour out a "New Move" upon all the earth, but the church is not yet ready to handle the magnitude of what God wants to release. God wants to pour out His glory upon His Church to touch the world. God is forming and preparing for Himself His spiritual army for the advance of His Kingdom. God wants to enlarge His people to be able to contain more of Him. There are great promises the Lord has given us. Promises of expansion, promises of enlargement, promises of greater reach into our communities and world. Isaiah 64:8 declares, "But now, O LORD, You are our Father; We are the clay, and You our potter; and all we are the work of Your hand."

Consider what 2 Timothy 2:21 says about our lives in the hands of the Potter: "Therefore if anyone cleanses himself from the latter, he will be a vessel for honor, sanctified and useful for the Master, prepared for every good work."

The Greek word used here for vessel is that of an item used for a specific purpose, or metaphorically, a body. It is the same word used in 2 Corinthians 4:7 which says God has put treasures in jars of clay—us! The treasures of His Kingdom and His glory have been deposited in our own lives. Indeed, our own lives and spirits are part of this great treasure in these "jars of clay." If we will keep ourselves pure and clean, if we will hate what is evil and love what is righteous, then God will pour out the golden oil of his joyous anointing on us *more than on anyone else* (Psalm 45:7), and God will use us for something honorable and beautiful beyond our comprehension. He is preparing us to be useful for His purposes.

THE HANDS OF THE POTTER

God is the Potter and we are the clay. He molds us into what He wants us to be. All of us have seen the picture or video of a potter sitting at the wheel with a mountain of clay. Upon preparing the clay, throwing in on the wheel, and spinning the table, the potter begins to form the clay. This clay is a work in progress. Our lives are equally a work in progress. We have the tendencies to think that we already know exactly what God wants to work in our lives and how He's going to do what He's going to do—even how He *should* be doing it! We are so sure about what God wants to do with us, but in reality we must not put God in our little boxes. God is the Potter and we are still in His process spinning around on His table. He has the ability to form, reform, or undo us in order to form something completely new. While we are still on His wheel and in His hands, we are still in process, and He can do with us whatever He wants. We must not limit Him. When we are on the Potter's wheel, and He is forming us; we cannot speed up His process in our lives. While we are waiting for the promise to be fulfilled, there is a way in which we must wait so that we will be adequately formed by Him.

4
THE HANDS OF THE POTTER

God is getting ready to pour out more of His presence, power, glory, and anointing in us, but as we are in this moment, we are incapable of receiving all of it. Before God can pour out everything He desires to give us, He needs to make our lives bigger so when He pours out His goodness upon us, He will find a Church which is prepared to advance with the New Move.

However, God has us both personally and corporately as His Church in a time of enlargement. Wait for Him and expect to see His hand moving your life. Expect challenges. Expect battles. Expect things to happen in your life that are going to obligate you to grow into a bigger person, a more mature person, and a person who is closer to the Lord than you ever have been before. As we go through difficult things in our lives, the Lord uses these things as a potter molds the clay. It is as if God is saying to us, "if you're with me, if you're ready, if you're available, I'm going to take you to another level of maturity."

When God sets Himself to do a New Move in the world, He needs people who are willing to be remade to fit His purposes for such a season. It is as if the Potter says to the clay, "Up to now your life has fulfilled My purposes, but now I need to reform you because I have another purpose for you." Then the Potter takes the clay pot and undoes it.

There are moments where we go through painful deconstructions in our lives. These are the moments when we most question God: "where are you? Why are you doing this to me?" God does not hate us—He is remaking us. There are certain things in our lives God needs to take out and others He needs to input in order to make us a larger vessel because He has larger purposes and larger anointing for our lives.

1 Peter 4:1-2 says, "Since Jesus went through everything you're going through and more, learn to think like Him. Think of your sufferings as a weaning from that old sinful habit of always expecting to get your own way. Then you'll be able to live out your days free to pursue what God wants instead of being tyrannized by what you

want" (The Message). The difficult and painful things in our lives are not God's wrath, they are the Potter's preparation of the clay for His purposes.

Our lives are works in process. We have the tendency to think we already know exactly what God is doing and how He is going to use our lives. Over 16 years of ministry, Teresa and I have had six different assignments. Each time the Lord moved us, I thought I knew and could predict about how long we would be there and how God would use us. I was *completely wrong* every time! The reality is that we cannot put God in our little boxes. He is the Potter and while we are still on His pottery wheel, He can form us, re-form us, and undo us to make us new. While we are on the wheel under His hands, we are in formation and He can do with us as He sees fit.

God needs to enlarge our way of thinking. I speak to you personally: stop saying God can't use you. Stop saying that your life isn't worthy. Stop saying you know everything and that you know exactly for what God made you and exactly how He's going to use your life. Stop saying that you know so much of the Bible, and you don't need any more spiritual formation, or you can afford to stop reading God's Word. These are lies to keep you nothing more than a small clay pot. While you are clay on the Potter's wheel, He can do with your life whatever He wants. If He wants to take your small clay pot and demolish it so He can re-create it into something completely new, He can do that to work greater maturity in us. Maybe this is precisely what He needs to do! When we feel God has undone us, or life squeezes us, and we even want to throw in the towel, don't do it! These are the moments when God's doing something new. It is something that requires more faith and more dependence upon Him, and more vision. In other words, God is leading you into a larger life so God can use you for his purposes in a greater way which requires more faith, more glory, and more of His presence. Your life is not your own, you are bought with a price by Jesus Christ and we are at His disposition.

God needs to enlarge our character. Stop sinning. Stop lying. A huge part of God's making us bigger is deciding it is no longer acceptable to live in sin. Sin and lies in all forms of dirtiness in our lives cannot contain God's glory. They cannot contain what God wants to do through our lives. God has placed us on this planet for only a certain amount of years to fulfill His purposes. We have no time to waste in sin, running from His calling, or disobeying Him. Be prepared! Fulfill the purpose for which He placed you here! Consider what Psalm 45:7 says:

"You love righteousness and hate wickedness;
Therefore God, Your God, has anointed You
With the oil of gladness more than Your
companions."

When there is hatred for sin and we live in righteousness, there is another dimension of anointing that God allows upon us.

God needs to enlarge our spiritual maturity. Advance in your faith! Advance and your understanding of the Bible! Advance in your ability to hear God's voice! There is no secret formula to advancing in faith and in hearing God's voice. It's asking. It's seeking. It's wanting. It's studying. It's committing yourself to the things of God. It's coming to church every time the doors are open. It's quieting yourself and listening. God does not have difficulty communicating with an open heart that is listening. We tend to have our ears filled with so much noise that we can't hear Him. Maybe we need to turn things off in our lives, to be with the Lord and just be quiet until He speaks. When He speaks, we'll grow faster and faster!

God needs to grow our desire for His presence. May God enlarge your prayer life. Call to Him for more of His presence and He will give it. May God enlarge your spiritual vision. May we love what He loves and hate what He hates. May we see the world around us with His eyes. May we be the clay pots on the Potter's wheel ready, willing, breakable, and available to become what God wants to make us.

5
WAITING

I want to explain what the word wait means in relationship to what God wants to do in our personal lives and in His Church. When we think of waiting, we tend to think of passing the time until it is our turn. Waiting has much more to do than simply "holding on" or "passing the time" or "staying put" until something happens.

Waiting has to do with expanding and preparing. Every person has a destiny for his or her life, but this destiny is not achieved immediately. We must wait, but this waiting carries with it the process of growth, preparation, and becoming. In order to go to the next level in education, we have to prepare and expand our capacity at the level in which we currently find ourselves—we cannot pass to the second grade until we have successfully achieved the merits of the first grade. If our goal is college, then to reach this goal, we must wait, but our waiting is not idle—it is quite active. We are "waiting" from Kindergarten through High School, all of which in part prepares us for the ultimate goal of college.

Waiting also carries the understanding of a pregnancy, which has the process of growth. When a woman is "waiting" for a baby, her body is expanding with the growth of the new life happening inside her, additionally the family is expanding in order to receive the baby. Maybe the family has to expand the house or move to somewhere bigger. But also their hearts are expanding with more room which will contain more love for a new member of the family. In the same way there are many preparations we must make in ourselves expand for the new life. Waiting has to do with preparation, expansion, and getting bigger.

While a woman has to wait for the birth of the baby and there is nothing she can do to force the arrival, but as she waits, she is anticipating and preparing everything the new baby will need.

Waiting patiently but with anticipation and preparation is exactly the way my wife was when she was pregnant with each of our four children. Every day when I got home from work, something else that was prepared: A wall painted, furniture rearranged, the crib put together with fresh sheets, baby clothes folded and put in the dresser drawer...there were lots of things being prepared! My wife was almost inexhaustible in her patient preparation. But when our babies arrived, a place was already prepared to receive them.

In the same way, the Church of Jesus Christ is "waiting" for new life—a New Move of His Spirit on the earth. God wants His Church to be prepared, to expand, to grow, to be bigger in order to birth the life God wants to give us, and in this way fulfill the purpose and destiny for which He called us into existence and for which he placed us in this time and season. But in order to fulfill His destiny, there must be a process of "waiting."

6
WAITING AND EXPECTATIONS

I want to make a distinction between waiting and expectation. They are similar in certain aspects and completely different in others. We note the similarity in the anticipation of something new. We can wait with great expectation. This is very natural! If you are waiting for a baby, you have a great expectation of new life, of joy, and a life filled with the wonder of this brand new little person. If you're waiting to open Christmas presents, you have the expectation of a joyous surprise upon opening the gift. We have reason we are to wait *expectantly*, but at the same time not we cannot require God to fulfill our own personal *expectations.*

In the wait, it is natural to have expectations of how something is going to be, how something is going to happen, or how something is going to look. There are parents who were, for a moment, disappointed at the birth of their child because it was not the gender they desired. There are children disappointed on Christmas morning because they did not receive the gifts that would have fulfilled their expectations. The period of waiting did not necessarily fulfill their expectation, and so when the moment came and the wait was over, they were unable to completely receive the new thing with gratitude and joy because it looked different than what they thought it *should* have looked like according to their own preconceived expectations.

FAITH AND TRAGEDY

There are times people do not receive the new work of God in their lives for the same reason. Perhaps a person is in the midst of tragedy or some other difficulty, then he or she cries out to God for intervention with the expectation that God is going to solve the issue with one fell swoop of His supernatural hand. But God responds according to what He sees, not necessarily according to what we think He ought to be doing or what we think we actually need.

At the time of this writing, it has been 16 years since my father suddenly passed away of a brain aneurysm. I was 22 years old, and he was only 49. As he lay in the hospital, literally 10's of thousands of people all around the world prayed for this amazing pastor of a very influential church to rise up and be healed. I was flooded with expectation of a miraculous healing, or a even a resurrection from the dead. All of our combined prayers would surely move Heaven and we *must* seen a miracle happen. Such was not just my expectation, but that of many thousands of people. Yet nothing happened. He went to be with the Lord with all our prayers seemingly hanging suspended between Heaven and earth unanswered.

I wrestled with this for quite a while. Why? Aren't you the God of miracles? Didn't you say that if we prayed for the sick, they would recover? Are you a fraud? Is everything I have believed a sham?

As I remembered all my experiences with the Lord over my life, I knew it wasn't a sham. Remembering all my encounters with the living God, I knew He wasn't a fraud. In a period of extended questioning and recounting, I asked myself, and knew that God is real, powerful, good, and caring—yet the worst happened.

This is where many people lose faith; when the reality of God doesn't fit their expectation of God. So if God is truly all these things, yet the worst happened, what, then, shall I put my faith in? It is not in His *power* to heal, because in this instance,

His power to heal did not meet my expectation of healing. Therefore, my faith needs to be place not in His *ability* to do something, but in His never-changing *character*: He is good. Regardless of the outcome; regardless of pain or sadness, happiness or joy, His character is good, and He is always working for the good of His people, even through our broken expectations.

A DIFFERENT RESPONSE TO EXPECTATIONS

In response to all the wickedness and pain in the world, God did not respond by throwing a divine atomic bomb to destroy all the wicked people of the world and leave only the good ones—which, by the way, is how many people think God ought to have done things. This is how human beings think, not God. Jesus' disciples literally wanted to do this very thing. When the enemy of the Jews, the Samaritans, did not let Jesus and the disciples pass through their city, two of the disciples asked Jesus if they could call down fire from heaven on the Samaritans! (See Luke 9:51-56).

God did not respond this way—nor does He respond this way. His response to the wickedness of the world was to send a baby. Wickedness is due to sin. But this baby came to destroy sin and destroy the works of the devil. For this same baby, there could not be found any room to be born among the people He came to save, and He had to be received among animals in a barn. When the religious scholars of the day were asked by King Herod about the appearance of the Messiah, they themselves, the very ones who should have had the expectancy, did not even bother to look.

When this same baby became a man, He was equally not well received. This Man could not possibly be the Messiah...He should be more kingly and overthrow all our Roman enemies! He was not received as Prophet, Priest, King, or the Son of God—and He was put to death. They could not see God's perfect plan though it was right there in front of them.

In the same way, we look for the spectacular answers from God, and isn't that right? Shouldn't the all powerful God respond with all of his might in every situation? *But God responds to us in a wholly different way. He gave the world a baby, and He gives us a seed.*

A seed looks absolutely nothing like our expectations. But this seed of the Kingdom of God begins to germinate in our hearts and works a deep transformation from the inside out. Many times, we are so focused on what we thought God *should be doing* according to our expectations, that we are blind to the much greater and deeper thing God *is doing* in our lives at this moment.

This was the ultimate point of the miracle of Jesus healing the blind man in John 9. The man who was born blind was twice healed. His physical and his spiritual eyes were opened. Yet those who were the religious bigwigs of the day were unable to understand either the miracle itself or the Son of God working in their midst. He who was blind could see because he received what God was doing, and those who could see were totally blind to the work of God because Jesus was not the way they thought the Messiah should be, and what is more, they were jealous of Him.

Envy and offense blind people's eyes to the works of God in whatever way God has chosen to reveal them. Therefore, when the Messiah stood right in front of them and worked the miracles of God, they couldn't see it was God Himself in their midst. I shudder to think how many times that has happened to me or to the Church of Jesus Christ. We have our human expectations and our tight theological boxes; our little 20 amp circuit breakers, or our too small clay pot. Our smallness and human expectations often times disallow us to move with the new thing God wants to do.

Jesus did not come in a way anyone expected Him, yet there were some who recognized the working of God in a little baby through poor nobodies like

Joseph and Mary. It is because those who could recognized Him were those who were lead by the Holy Spirit.

JESUS IS IN THE LEAST OF THESE

In Matthew 25:31-46, Jesus tells us a parable of the sheep and the goats—or, as we understand from the parable, the faithful and unfaithful people who are being judged by King Jesus. Both are judged by their responses to the same thing which is how they treated Jesus when He was right in front of them. The "sheep" (faithful people) and the "goats" (unfaithful people) both asked when they served, loved, and provided for [or not] Jesus Himself. Jesus said to them, "When you did it (or not) for the least of these, you did it unto Me."

I wonder how many times Jesus has been in front of us and we did not have the spiritual insight to see Him. I wonder how many times we have turned our backs on Jesus when we mistreated someone in our church, refused to buy a hungry person dinner after church, did not care for the pregnant mother who had a tough pregnancy, or shared the Gospel with someone God had placed right in front of us. I wonder how many times Jesus was not recognized and served even among His own people today. Many of us swear we will never be like the rigid, religious, legalistic, and spiritually blind Pharisees of Jesus' time—but are we? Do we see Jesus in "the least of these"?

But Simeon and Ana recognized Jesus. They did not see a mighty warrior, a conquering King, or anything that would give away the fact that He was the Son of God, no. They recognized Him immediately in an eight-day-old baby. They were spiritually astute and saw immediately the way that God subtly—almost imperceptibly—comes among His people to deliver them. I find it of great importance that the two people who were in prayer, in the Temple, and lead by the Spirit were the ones who recognized Jesus. I pray that all of us are equally as spiritually alert as we give ourselves to prayer.

This was true back in Jesus' time, and it is still true in our time today. Jesus worked the works of God in front of the religious people of the day, and they could not see past their religious jealousy. Today, the same small-mindedness persists in a religious spirit. When God moves through people or churches, the religious spirit of contention, debate, jealousy, legalism, self-righteousness, and criticism rears its ugly head against any new move of God. But walking closely with the Holy Spirit will allow us to see God's true working for what it is and rejoice in it!

We do not have any control over the gender or the features of a baby, nor do we have control over the gifts that somebody gives us a Christmas, and we certainly cannot control the way God does or does not decide to move. We only have to wait with the anticipation of something new. We do not have the right to require God to make things to look like we want them to be. At the end of the day, the main point of God's working is not *how* He is going to do it, but *what* He is actually doing right now. We wait with great anticipation for what God is going to do but without the preconceived expectation of how God will make it happen.

Many people allow themselves to be led by their expectations so much that they lose the blessing that is in front of their face or the process which God is bringing about in their lives. It is not okay to desire a spouse so much that in a moment of desperation you go and marry the first person who winks at you. Such a person does not know how to wait, only fulfill an expectation that they thought was too long in coming. This person's expectation is so focused on what they want that he or she couldn't see that God first wanted to prepare their lives for the better thing He had in store.

There are moments when God doesn't seem to be moving fast enough. Moments of our frustration and anger. Moments of sadness and moments of feeling stuck. What we can do these moments? Most of us try to "make it happen"; we try to force an issue. We talk or act at the wrong time and mess up a potential opportunity. We allow our emotions to control us and we begin to assuage our frustrations with vice. We "golden calf it." As Abraham John so aptly put in his book *Keys to Passing Your Spiritual Test* regarding the incident with the Golden Calf:

"They became impatient, took their life in their own hands, and began to play God. There will be times in our life when...things will not always happen the way we want or when we want...When we fail the test of delayed gratification and fail to wait for God's timing, we always get into something that is not God's perfect will. When we step out to do something that is not in conjunction with the will of God for our lives, it will bring situations and results that we cannot easily get rid of, or things we did not expect or want in the first place will suddenly manifest."

But we have the promise that if we will "wait upon the Lord...We will run and not grow weary." And God will, "in due season open his hand and satisfy" our desires—but He always does it on His terms and in His time.

7
PRAYER THAT BRINGS THE HOUSE DOWN

After centuries of unfaithfulness to God, God had permitted the southern tribes of Israel to be taken captive by the Babylonians. Yet with their captivity came the promise of the return of a remnant to Israel. The punishment of their captivity was to last seventy years, according to the prophet Jeremiah (Jeremiah 29:10).

The ministry of the prophet Daniel endured through the entire seventy years of captivity. As Daniel read through the book of the prophet Jeremiah, he realized that the seventy years were almost over. Daniel records his actions, "In the first year of his reign I, Daniel, understood by the books the number of the years specified by the word of the LORD through Jeremiah the prophet, that He would accomplish seventy years in the desolations of Jerusalem. Then I set my face toward the Lord God to make request by prayer and supplications, with fasting, sackcloth, and ashes." (Daniel 9:2-3).

When the time for deliverance and fulfillment came, Daniel's response was to pray—to pray hard. Daniel understood that his prayers were essential in the unleashing of God's move and for the fulfillment of destiny. Intense prayer and intentional intercession which free people from bondage, move the hand of God, and release people into their destinies are prayers that bring the house down.

There are seasons when it is time to push hard— this is true spiritually just as it is physically. When speaking of the End Times, Jesus likened them to the labor pains of a woman about to give birth (Matthew 24:8). A woman does not know exactly when the child is going to be born, but when the labor pains get hard enough, painful enough, and frequent enough, she knows the time has come to push hard for the baby to be born.

The same is true in the spiritual realm. The signs of the times, like birth pains, are clear warnings for us to begin to push in prayer—and push hard! This is what Daniel was doing in his intercession: He was birthing Israel's freedom in prayer. Consider what happens if we do not see the signs of the times and do not pray for the move of God to be birthed among us. If a woman will not push out the baby, the baby's life is in jeopardy.

Likewise, in the time of the prophet Ezekiel, God was going to pour out judgment upon Israel and God declares to the prophet in Ezekiel 22:30, "...I sought for a man among them who would make a wall, and stand in the gap before Me on behalf of the land, that I should not destroy it; but I found no one." The implication is that since no one stood before the Lord in prayer and intercession, though God was willing to relent on behalf of His people, disaster was released instead. God is ready to move on our earth. Will you rise up and pray for a mighty move of His Spirit in these last days?

Two Cups

There is a principle we find in the Bible of "the measure of iniquity" where God's judgment becomes imminent when the measure of sin is too great to continue to *not* do something. This is true of Nebuchadnezzar, over whom judgment was pronounced for the overwhelming measure of his stubborn, insolent pride (Daniel 4:28-33), as well as his successor Belshazzar who saw the handwriting on the wall. For Belshazzar, the handwriting said, "...you have been weighed in the balances and have not measured up..." (Daniel 5:27 NLT). Interestingly, when God shows Abraham the land his descendents will inherit, God says, "In the fourth generation your descendants will come back here, for the sin of the Amorites has not yet reached its full measure (Genesis 15:16), with another translation saying, "...the sins of the Amorites do not yet warrant their destruction" (NLT). Jesus said that the measure with which we mete out to others is the measure which we ourselves will receive (Matthew 7:2). Finally, we see this in the Great Prostitute of Babylon in the book of Revelation 16:19 who drank the cup of the blood of the saints, and in its place she was given the cup of God's wrath as punishment for her brazen sin and ruthless cruelty. Here, the measure is depicted as in a cup. There comes a point when the cup overflows.

Yet there is another cup. Psalm 23:5 says, "You prepare a table before me in the presence of my enemies; You anoint my head with oil; my cup runs over." Here, we see a cup running over with blessings from the Lord, not judgment! In Romans 5:20, Paul says that where sin's measure increases, the measure of God's grace increases much more. Not that we should keep sinning to experience more of God's grace, but that God's grace is big enough to forgive.

The Cup of Sin and the Cup of Grace are both filling up. I believe the Cup of Grace fills much more quickly than that of sin. But if we will not intercede for our city, state, nation, and world, the Cup of Sin will overflow, as in Ezekiel 22:30. Praying the house down is filling the Cup of God's Grace. I want to see an overflow of that!

PRAY THROUGH THE SEASONS

There are seasons in your life, too. There are moments where things are happening in the lives of your children, in your job, or in your own soul that require, like Daniel, an ear for what God is doing to intervene with His Kingdom and restoration. We understand what God is doing through the Scripture, through waiting on Him and listening for the voice of His Spirit, and through attentiveness to the signs in our own lives. We then partner with Him and pray hard until what God wants to do comes about. But it will not come about without the participation of our prayers!

Do not give up in prayer and intercession for your children! Do not give up in prayer and intercession for your marriage! Do not give up in prayer and intercession for the fullness of God's work in your life and destiny! God is moving in the world—and He is moving in your family too. Pray it in!

TWO HOUSE-DOWN INTERCESSORS

The Bible tells us of the most important move of

God in the history of the world. "When the fullness of the time had come, God sent forth His Son" (Galatians 4:4). God had set everything in place, and now was His time to move among humanity as never before.

In the story of Jesus' birth, there are two people who most people forget, yet these two people had much to do with the ushering in of the greatest moves of God our world has ever seen—the birth of our Savior, Jesus Christ. These two people are Simeon and Anna.

Simeon was a "just and devout" man who was waiting for Israel's Messiah to come. It is important to note the Scriptures also say that he was a man *upon* whom was the Holy Spirit, and the Spirit *revealed* to him that he would see the Christ, the Messiah, before he died, and he was *moved* by the Holy Spirit to go to the Temple on the day Jesus was being presented to God (Luke 2:25-28).

SIMEON AND THE COMING OF CHRIST
Simeon was "waiting" for the redemption of Israel. As we talked about before, the word "waiting" does not mean he was laying around on the couch lazily waiting for the possibility that something was going to happen. Simeon's waiting was an active, hopeful waiting for the fulfillment of God's

promises.

When God wants to bring new life—or a New Move—into our world, He is looking for a place that is prepared to receive this new life; a place of patient, active, anticipative waiting. Simeon both waited for God's salvation and was lead into the fulfillment of God's promise by the Holy Spirit. As Psalm 25:5 declares, "Lead me in Your truth and teach me, For You are the God of my salvation; On You I wait all the day."

Simeon was waiting in this same way. He desired, sought for, and hungered to see the completion of God's promise. The Scripture in Luke 2:25-28 does not explicitly say it, but you can rest assured that Simeon's waiting was in prayer and intercession for the fulfillment of what the Holy Spirit had revealed to him about the coming of the Messiah. When God reveals things to us through His Word, in visions, dreams, or in prophecy, the purpose is not for us speculate or tell everyone on Facebook, Twitter, and post a prophetic picture on Instagram—it is to pray. Revelation and intercession go hand-in-hand. Revelation which moves into intercessory prayer is how we begin to pray the house down!

In this same passage of Scripture, three times it mentions the Holy Spirit in conjunction with

Simeon. The Bible reveals that the Holy Spirit was ***upon*** him, ***revealing*** to him what God intended to do in the world through the coming of the Messiah, and ***leading*** him to the Temple to see the completion of God's plan. The Holy Spirit wants to guide our intercession in the same way.

As we pray and intercede for our family, friends, church, nation, and world, the Holy Spirit needs to take the central role. We must permit Him to dwell among us as He rested upon Simeon. As His presence is welcomed among people whose ears are attending to His voice, and whose hearts are tender to His direction, He will guide us in how to pray and intercede. Guidance is one of the essential ministries of the Holy Spirit. Jesus said in John 16:13 that the Holy Spirit will "guide you into all truth." As the Holy Spirit revealed to Simeon what was to come, the Holy Spirit will guide us into how we are to pray for God's New Move on the earth.

Finally, as the Holy Spirit lead Simeon into the right place at the right time to see the fulfillment of God's promise, as we pray, intercede, and listen for the voice of the Spirit, He will lead us into everything He has promised and fulfill ***in*** us and ***through*** us everything He desires to do in the world all ***around*** us.

ANNA AND THE COMING OF JESUS

After Simeon encountered the promise by seeing the baby Jesus, the prophetess Anna arrived on the scene, knowing, too, the Messiah had come. The Bible tells us that she was a widow for eighty-four years and that she dedicated herself to prayers and fasting everyday in the Temple—she almost never left the Temple area. The biblical passage does not tell us for what she was praying and fasting, but the context of the story does. She, as Simeon, was waiting, praying, and fasting for the coming of the Messiah, (Luke 2:36-38).

Anna was a fervent intercessor. The Greek word used for Anna's prayers is used for intense supplications. Anna's requests and intercession was for God to intervene in the affairs of the world. We see with both Simeon and Anna, they exhibit the characteristics of intercession that moves the heart and hand of God. They both interceded for the plan of God in Jesus Christ to come to pass in the world. Their intercession, I believe, is part of the reason Jesus came when He did. It was in God's plan, and there were at least two people who brought it to pass in prayer.

PRAYER AND REVIVAL

Their intercession is part of the reason Jesus arrived when he arrived. Perhaps this is a little bit much to process or even fully believe. After all, didn't God already have the time planned for Jesus to come? Of course he did. But that does not negate the fact that He needs His people to cry out to Him in intercession until His plan is fulfilled. "But isn't God sovereign?" we ask. "He is eternal and all powerful. He can do whatever He wants whenever He wants. The omnipotent God surely didn't rely on Simeon and Anna," we argue. Of course God *can* do as He pleases, but God made a decision *in His sovereignty* about how life would be between Him and humanity. He sovereignly decided to work with and through us.

As John Wesley famously said, "God does nothing on the earth save in response to human prayer." When the Lord told Elijah the rains were going to come, Elijah fervently prayed until they came—Elijah's prayers were the impetus for the unfolding of the miracle (2 Kings 18:41-46). Jesus even told us to pray this way, that what is going on in Heaven would be made manifest on the earth (Matthew 6:10).

Twice God told Moses He was going to destroy the Israelites in the desert and start all over with him (first with the Golden Calf incident, and the second with the bad report of the ten spies incident), yet Moses' intercession for the people held back God's hand and God relented (Exodus 32:12-14; Numbers 14:11-20). And as we already saw in the book of Ezekiel, God searches for a man who would "stand in the gap" so God would relent of the judgment He had planned, but He found no one, therefore the judgment came, though it came unwillingly on God's part. God wanted—no, needed—someone to stop Him, and there were none If there was an intercessor things would have been different, (Ezekiel 22:30).

We want to see movement of God among us. A move of God primarily begins with prayer and intercession. Revival does not happen just because it is announced in a church for a few nights; rather revival ignites when the people of God begin to live in purity and holiness and begin to cry out to Him for an intervention in His Church. God has us in His process and in His time of "waiting." It is like the Church is pregnant. We cannot hurry the process. But what are we doing in the meantime to prepare adequately? We wait upon the Lord, but we are waiting actively! Pray, Church! God is going to answer!

8
WHEN THE HOUSE COMES DOWN

Simeon and Anna prayed the house down for the coming of the Messiah—and it happened. The Messiah, Jesus Christ, came announcing the rule of a new Kingdom that would destroy the work of the devil (1 John 3:8). Jesus did fulfill the expectation of the first century Jews, but in a way they did not expect. Their expectation was to be delivered from the tyranny of the Romans, but Jesus delivered them from the far worse tyranny of sin. Though Simeon and Anna did not know it at the time, they helped light a fuse that caused worldwide explosion—an that explosion brought the house down!

As Jesus came of age and began His earthly ministry, His work did not go farther than the boarders of Israel. There were times when He ministered to Gentiles, but Jesus said that He was "sent to the lost sheep of the house of Israel" (Matthew 15:24). Yet we also know from the revelation of the Scriptures, both in the Old and New Testaments, that God's ultimate plan of salvation includes all the nations of the world. These two seemingly incompatible statements have a reason behind them.

In Jesus Christ, God entered the human arena; He became flesh. As Jesus walked on the earth, He was both Son of God and Son of Man. Though He did not cease to be the Son of God, He lived as the Son of Man. He was—and continues to be for all eternity—human. Jesus was filled with the power of the Holy Spirit and did miracles, signs, and wonders, but He was still a man. He was not omnipresent or all-powerful. He was human like you and me.

Jesus' ministry did not end with His resurrection or with His ascension back into Heaven, no. It not end—*it exploded*. After His ascension, Jesus' ministry went much farther than Jesus Himself could have spread it. Shortly before His crucifixion, Jesus told His disciples that it was to their advantage that He go away; if He did not go away, He would not be able to send the Holy Spirit to the Believers. Jesus knew that He had come to *redeem* humanity, but He also knew that He came to *empower* humanity.

John the Baptist proclaimed that One was coming after him and He [Jesus] will "...baptize you with the Holy Spirit and fire" (Luke 3:16). Moving closer to the end of His ministry, Jesus, longing for the explosion and greater outbreak of His ministry, said, "I came to send fire on the earth, and how I wish it were already kindled!" (Luke 12:49). The fire Jesus spoke of was the fire of the empowerment of the Holy Spirit burning in all believers. Jesus knew that when He sent the Holy Spirit, there would be a worldwide explosion of ministry by Heaven's power touching the earth through His people.

Jesus announced to His followers, "he who believes in Me, the works that I do he will do also; and greater works than these he will do, because I go to My Father," (John 14:12). We are the Body of Christ—sons and daughters of man whom have become the sons and daughters of God filled with His Spirit to do the same things that the Son of God and Man did. In this way, Jesus' ministry expanded by living in us through His Spirit!

A WORLDWIDE EXPLOSION
Right before Jesus went to the Father to unleash the Holy Spirit upon all believers, He instructed His disciples saying,

[Do not] depart from Jerusalem, but to wait
for the Promise of the Father, "which,"
Jesus said, "you have heard from Me; for
John truly baptized with water, but you
shall be baptized with the Holy Spirit not
many days from now." (Acts 1:4-5)

From the time of Jesus' ascension back to the
Father until the Holy Spirit was poured out upon
them on the day of Pentecost, the followers of
Jesus met in the Upper Room. They were in unity
together and they were praying—and praying
hard. These were not the short prayers we are
accustomed to making. These were prayers that
lasted for hours-on-end with intense supplication.
If it were anything else, Luke, the author of Acts,
would have no need to mention it.[1]

What were Jesus' followers praying about in that
Upper Room? We can surmise that they were
praying for the very thing Jesus had promised
them: The coming of the Holy Spirit. Though it is
doubtful they fully understood what the coming of
the Spirit was going to look like, all the disciples
had to hang on to was Jesus' last instruction to
them not to leave until the Holy Spirit baptized
them. And then it happened: The Holy Spirit

---

[1] Keener, Craig. Bible Background Commentary: New Testament. InterVarsity Press. (Downers Grove: 1993), 325

came and _**everything**_ changed.

I find a wonderful symmetry in the prayers of Simeon and Ana and the disciples: They all prayed in a New Move of God—they all brought the House down, first with Jesus, then with the Holy Spirit! The worldwide explosion began with the pouring out of God's power upon the believers. It is not coincidental that the Holy Spirit came during a prayer meeting.

I also find that we have a wonderful symmetry to fulfill in these times. Simeon and Anna were in intense prayer, fasting, and intercession before Jesus came the first time. Just as there was a passionate anticipation of the coming of the Messiah in the first century, there is an equally passionate anticipation that is growing among God's people for the Second Coming of Jesus Christ. *If powerful house-down prayer was offered before Jesus' First Coming, then you and I should offer equally powerful prayer before Jesus' Second Coming! Let's bring down the house!*

You and I are Simeon and Ana! We are Jesus' disciples! God answers us when we call out to Him, and His Holy Spirit begins to move in our midst when we are open and available to Him, submitted to His lordship, and grounded in God's Word. Pray! Lift up your voice before God! Cry out for His coming! Cry out for many millions of souls to be saved in these last days! Cry out for the New Move of His Spirit!

THE WORK OF THE HOLY SPIRIT
God is looking for people who will allow the work of the Holy Spirit in their midst. He seeks people who will not dismiss it out of ignorance, ignore it out of fear, or abuse it out of fleshliness—but in simple, child-like openness, will allow God to come in and do what He desires to do.

Some years ago, there was a particular Wednesday night where God released healing in the congregation I pastored at the time. I had not anticipated this sudden move of God's Spirit among us, but something unusual happened before that particular service.

A young man, who had been overcome with alcoholism, contacted me. He was in front of a liquor store weeping. Everything of his flesh craved another drink, but he was tired of this bondage and wanted to be free. There was an enormous struggle in him. He had texted me, and I immediately called him back. I told him to come to the church, and I began to pray for him. As I ministered to him, I began to cry out from the depth of my being for "Jesus the Healer" to come and set this man free. Over and over I groaned and shouted that Jesus the Healer would come. After many minutes of prayer and ministry, we ended and prepared for that evening's service.

During the worship time, the Holy Spirit impressed upon my heart that there was a river of healing flowing in our congregation and that God was there to heal people. This was unexpected, but I obeyed the Lord and stepped up to the platform and began to call for anyone who was infirm to come forward to be prayed for. About half the congregation stepped forward and the Lord touched many people. As I and the other pastors were praying with people, the Lord spoke to my heart as to why there was a river of healing available: Because I had been calling out to Jesus the Healer before service. In calling upon Jesus, He came to heal!

Just as the disciples gathered in the Upper Room, and Simeon and Anna constantly cried out to God in the Temple, and they all saw a move of God in their midst as they prayed, God will also respond with a move of His Spirit as we pray for this New Move. It is the job of the Church to reach the lost—we need to pray that God will give them to us. It is the job of the Church to intercede for our city, state, country, and world—we need to pray for a move of God among us. It is the job of the Church to disciple people and minister to them—

we need to pray for the Holy Spirit to give us the spirit of wisdom and revelation (Ephesians 1:17). We need to pray for the outpouring of God's mighty works of miracles, healing, and the fruitful operation of the gifts of the Holy Spirit among us and through us. If we will pray, God will move among us. If we will pray, God will pour out His Holy Spirit afresh upon us. If we will pray, God will ignite a New Move in our land!

9
THE HOUSE COMES DOWN
ALL THROUGH HISTORY

I want to take into some historical context the times in which we live and what God is preparing for. We have inherited a world with many problems and polemics that only God can solve. These problems were made and expounded by the choices of sinful humanity. God is at work in our world, and I am supremely hopeful of an outbreak of His Spirit not long from now. At the same time, God has been at work in our world for a long time, and He is drawing things toward an ultimate conclusion.

Nothing that happens in the world today happened in a vacuum; all things are the way they are for specific reasons that past events have dictated. We are the inheritors of history, yet God is the Lord of all history. All time is in His hands and He is moving history itself toward a final conclusion. As inheritors of history, it is our job to steward the present and pray the House down for future history to be set on a godly course—the way we do that is by praying as agents and ambassadors of the Kingdom of God to intersect, intervene, and interpose itself on our temporary, earthly realm. In other words, the most kingly, powerful, and history-shaping thing we can do is to pray and intercede the house down! Think of it: We can impact the present, oversee and govern events, and shape the future by the way we pray.

Jesus tells us a parable about the end of history in Matthew 13:24-30:

"The kingdom of heaven is like a man who sowed good seed in his field; but while men slept, his enemy came and sowed tares among the wheat and went his way. But when the grain had sprouted and produced a crop, then the tares also appeared. So the servants of the owner came and said to him, 'Sir, did you not sow good seed in your field? How then does it have tares?' He said to them, 'An enemy has done this.' The servants said to him, 'Do you want us then to go and gather them up?' But he said, 'No, lest while you gather up the tares you also uproot the wheat with them. Let both grow together until the harvest, and at the time of harvest I will say to the reapers, "First gather together the tares and bind them in bundles to burn them, but gather the wheat into my barn."

Later on in the chapter Jesus plainly interprets the parable for His disciples. The sower is Jesus, the field is the world, the good seed are the sons of the Kingdom of God, the weeds are the people of the evil one and the enemy who sowed the weeds is the devil, the harvest is the end of the age, and the harvesters are the angels. Now that the scene is set, let's take a quick look at human history in light of Jesus' parable.

GOD'S WORK IN HISTORY
Throughout human history, there has always been good and evil at work in humanity. In Genesis 3:15, after the fall of mankind into sin, God pronounces His first judgment upon the serpent saying, "I will put enmity between you and the woman, and between your seed and her seed." From the very beginning, God designates good and evil as seed. The ultimate seed of the woman, Jesus Christ, will crush the serpent. But the fact remains that the serpent has seed, too. The seed of the woman will produce a Savior through whom humanity can be saved. Yet those who oppose God and persecute

God's people are the "seed" of the serpent.

The whole story of the Bible is of God working in history to "destroy the works of the devil" and recover the lost, damaged human race (1 John 3:8). In Jesus' parable we see the basic reality of God's good and the devil's evil at war with one another among humanity. Both "seeds"—the good and the evil—are growing together. We see in our world the reality of this parable. Evil has been defeated by the cross, but it has not yet been eradicated from our world: It is maturing, and coming to a head along with God's Kingdom.

The battlefield is the world and the prize is the souls of all the people in the human race. Jesus, explaining about the end of the age, teaches, "But as the days of Noah were, so also will the coming of the Son of Man be." We know of the times of Noah that "the wickedness of man was great in the earth, and that every intent of the thoughts of his heart was only evil continually," (Matthew 24:37; Genesis 6:5). Until Jesus' Second Coming and the final harvest, both good and evil will mature and ripen along side each other.

A LITTLE-CHANGING WORLD
For many thousands of years, human beings lived much the same way on the earth. Of course there were technological, agricultural, and artistic

breakthroughs, but they were several millennia in the making. I am not going to argue here the age of humanity, but whether you believe humanity is only several millennia old or millions of years old, it makes little difference to the point of this chapter, however, it is generally agreed upon by historians that the world did not transition out of the Stone Age until somewhere between 6000 – 2500 BC.

Even through the transition of ages from Stone, to Bronze, to Iron, all the way through to the Middle Ages, with all the technological advances of military weapons and architecture, the reality is that life changed very little for most of the world during all those millennia. Cities were still laid out much the same, farming and animal herding were much the same, and warfare was much the same (whether you use stone weapons are iron weapons, many of the tactics remain the same).

THE WORLD CHANGES…FAST!
Not until the Late Middle Ages did the world begin to change more rapidly than it ever had before since the beginning of human history. By the early to middle 1300's Europe began to experience what came to be known as The Renaissance, or re-birth, which would last until roughly 1700.

Before we go on, I want to put into perspective how staggering this is: Out of the thousands or even millions of years from humanities creation, the modern world did not begin to come into existence until only 700 years ago!

The western world, which went on to form much of the world we know today, experienced marvelous advances in art with names such a Da Vinci and Michelangelo; development of modern political theoretical concepts of both communism and the freedoms of our American democratic republic; significant advances in medicine and science and military weaponry; with the first brass cannon being produced in Florence, Italy in 1321. This weapon was of massive significance because it changed the way warfare was conducted. When you change warfare, you change tactics. When you change tactics, you change the way cities are laid out and this changes the way people live.

Never before in the history of the world had so many significant leaps forward been made so rapidly. Yet the Church had been dominant since the Roman Emperor Constantine converted to Christianity 312 AD. Only a few decades later, by 380 AD, Christianity was made the official religion of the Roman Empire.

The end of the Middle Ages and the re-birth of the

Renaissance was the beginning of the modern, secular world in which we live today. The Renaissance was the foundation fro a much more secularized world. Though not completely separate from the influence of the Church, the scientific, medical, political, and intellectual communities began separating from the domination the Church held for the previous 1000 years.

THE WHEAT AND THE WEEDS BEGIN TO MATURE
During the 1000 years of domination, the Church became corrupt with political might, military power, extravagant wealth, and a much diluted Gospel. Yet on the fringes of history we see God still moving through His Church in the face of a dark time in Church history.

As an extraordinary example of the times, the humble, pious, and self-sacrificing St. Francis of Assisi was visiting the Pope in Rome. The Pope, who is purported to sit in St. Peter's seat as the "rock on which Jesus built the Church," and the Bishop of Rome, showed him all the Vatican's vast wealth. He pridefully said to Francis, "Peter can no longer say, 'Silver and gold have I none!'" To which St. Francis replied, "Neither can he say, 'rise up and walk.'"

A simplified, broad sweeping explanation of the

pulling away of the fast-changing culture from the influence of the Church was much due to the fact that the Church did not embrace the new scientific and technological advances yet desired to hold absolute power over the culture.

During the Renaissance and the rise of the modern, secular culture, we see a great New Move of the Holy Spirit begin with a Catholic monk named Martin Luther. Luther challenged the Church which had strayed from the Gospel by selling salvation to raise money for St. Peter's Basilica in Rome. God, through Luther, brought a New Move of returning to the biblical teaching of salvation through faith alone in Christ alone.

Juxtaposed to the secular Renaissance comes the great Reformation of the Church on October 31, 1517. Along with Martin Luther and the rise of the Protestant Church, the Holy Spirit was moving in the Catholic Church with Ignatius Loyola who birthed the Jesuit movement in 1534, which became one of the most successful missionary movements in the history of the Church. With these two movements, the Renaissance and the Reformation, we see the Jesus' parable of the Wheat and the Weeds start coming to fruition—both the wheat of the Reformation and the weeds of the Renaissance are growing together.

THE AGE OF REASON AND THE GREAT AWAKENING
Over the previous three centuries, we see the clear growth and maturation of the wheat and the weeds. The beliefs and worldview that began to prevail upon the world were becoming decidedly anti-Christ while, at the same time, the Holy Spirit began a New Move as never before upon the earth. When the period of the Renaissance ended, the world was thrust into the Age of Enlightenment, which is also known as the Age of Reason, which lasted from 1650 to 1790.

The Age of Reason was the glorification of the human ability to think. There is nothing wrong with thinking and reasoning, God gave us brilliant minds to use them to the fullest. However, the glorification of humanity was a leap forward in the human race believing that we could supplant God's wisdom and usurp His place, indeed, even do away with Him completely. Why? Because we were now smart enough and enlightened enough with science and reason to the point where God was becoming little more than an antiquated idea.

Whereas many of the great names of the Renaissance were men of the Church, the great names of the Enlightenment became far more detached from religious thinking. Many of these people were Deist rather than Christian. A Deist is one who believes in God as Creator, but maintains that God is detached and disinterested in the world, therefore human reason now reigns supreme.

With the prevailing worldview of the dominant culture pulling ever farther away from God, the Holy Spirit stirred up a New Move in the American Colonies with revival fire. From 1731 to 1755, this revival became known as the First Great Awakening. God moved through men like John Wesley, George Whitfield, and Jonathan Edwards. In an age where reason trumped spirituality, people flocked to the Gospel, cried out in repentance, and many were filled with the power of the Holy Spirit.

The Great Revolutions

Toward the latter side of the Age of Reason, revolutions all over the world began to break out from around 1760 to 1820. There was the French Revolution, which was active in running the Church out of France, in contrast to the American Revolution, which founded the nation that was instrumental in advancing the Gospel worldwide; and the Industrial Revolution, which gave rise to vast leaps forward in the development of science, technology, manufacturing, and the migration of millions of people from the rural farm to populate cities. Once again, the pace of world change was quickening and the gap between secular worldview and religious worldview continued to widen.

With all the reasoning, scientific advances, and revolutions, God, once again, sovereignly did a New Move by His Spirit upon the world. This revival took place from about 1790 to 1840, and it became known as the Second Great Awakening in the newly formed and independent United States. Once again, people came to the Gospel in droves. This fervent revivalism sprang up in direct response to the hyper-rationalism of the day. People, again, repented and were filled with the Holy Spirit.

The Second Great Awakening gave rise to fervent voluntarism and missionary work. As a result of this revival, prayer, intercession, and people coming to Christ, missionaries were sent from the United States all around the world as never before; the common person began to advance the cause of the Gospel in his or her everyday life; and issues such as women's rights, the abolition of slavery, and temperance came to the forefront of society. At the beginning of the Second Great Awakening, church attendance in the United States was 5%-7%. Roughly hundred years later, in the early 1900's, church attendance had rise to a staggering 50%![2]

Shortly after the Second Great Awakening, different assaults on the Gospel occurred. Darwin's theory of evolution gave society yet another reason to take more steps away from our Creator. In the late 1800's we see the surge of sects such as the Mormons, Scientology, and Jehovah's Witnesses begin to distort the Gospel of Jesus Christ. In the early 1900's, the Bolshevik Revolution in Russia occurred and the rise of the anti-God, communist state which, in turn, initiated the Iron Curtain in Eastern Europe and the radical persecution of Christians after World War 2.

The farther society strays from God, the more fervent the New Moves of these End Times have become—***the wheat and weeds mature together.*** In a time where many attacks on the Gospel were made, and I have only mentioned a few, God poured out His Sprit significantly in Wales and in Los Angeles, CA. The Welsh Revival of 1904 and 1905 swept across Wales, Britain, Scandinavia, and mainland Europe. In 1906, the Azusa Street Revival broke out in Los Angles, CA. The scope of this revival was such as the world had not seen since the days when the first century believers swept through the Roman world.

---

[2] Garlow, James. God and His People, Victor Books, Colorado Springs, 2004, chapters 13-16

This revival of people coming to Jesus Christ and being baptized with the Holy Spirit launched into a worldwide revival. In 1945, a full forty years after the outbreak of the Azusa Street Revival, Pentecostals numbers about 16 million.[3] By the year 2005, Pentecostals numbered 600 million![4]

A NEW REVOLUTION—AND A NEW MOVE
The world continues to change today. There was a great thrust forward in the evolution of culture and societal values during the Renaissance, and with each subsequent era, the pace has quickened. Each era of maturation has been the foundation for the next, and they are growing toward the ultimate harvest. But each outpouring of God's Spirit has also been the foundation for the next.

Another sign of the maturation of the wheat and the weeds happened in the 1960's with the Hippie movement and the Sexual Revolution. Almost nothing else in American history has more deteriorated the state of the culture in which we live today than the Sexual Revolution. The acceptable ideas that sex was a wild free-for-all with no commitment or sense of morality needed; that drugs were a mind-expander to be enjoyed;

---

[3] Garlow, 469-470
[4] Synan, Vinson
http://enrichmentjournal.ag.org/200602/200602_142_legacies.cfm

and the twisted, self-indulgent, perverted idea that love should be defined as whatever makes you happy; and the relativism of never being so narrow-minded so as to challenge anyone else's concept of love, so you can simply do as you please with no consequences. If you question anyone else—or worse, you don't conform to the cultural norm—you are intolerant and you hate. Such a movement shifted thinking around the world toward a mature, ripe weed.

Unsurprisingly, along with the Sexual Revolution, there was another New Move of the Holy Spirit in the midst of the culture. In 1960, the Charismatic Renewal began at a small Episcopal Church in Van Nuys, CA, with Father Dennis Bennett. The Charismatic Renewal swept around the world over the subsequent decades. Also, In 1968, in Costa Mesa, CA, a movement spontaneously broke out among Hippies who were disillusioned with their failed worldview, and they began to come to Christ—this movement was called The Jesus People.

THE WORLD TODAY
We face challenges in our world today that perhaps are not new, but they are accelerated and more widespread than at any other time in human history. I believe, as do many millions of believers around the world, that we are in the End Times

and that Jesus' return is imminent.

As a result of these rapid changes over the last 700 years of human history, secular society has become unequivocally anti-Christ. Jesus likened the signs of the end to a woman going into labor (Matthew 24:8). There have been signs of the End Times since Jesus resurrection, but in the last 100 years, and especially in the last 60 years, the contractions are getting harder, more frequent and more painful.

The LGBTQ revolution over the last 20 years has been the inevitable, ugly child of the weed-seed. Homosexuality has become acceptable—even celebrated—as have the aborting of unborn children under the veil of women's rights to choose, and to live in unbridled promiscuity. The over-sexed, tolerant-of-everything-except-Jesus culture, has allowed the LGBTQ agenda and the progressive, humanistic, relativistic, Leftist worldview to encircle the globe and capture the hearts and minds of 100's of millions of people with demonic fury—and that is exactly what it is: Demonic, not political.

With equal demonic fury, Islam has come to the forefront of current history. With adherents to Islam projected to rival, maybe even surpass, those of Christianity, the threat of what this world might become over the next few decades is a terrifying thought. The "Arab Spring" in the Middle East in 2010 which gave place to more radical Islam, and the Leftist worldview held by the prevailing culture that prefers the acts of Islam to the saving power of Jesus, has set the world stage. The weeds are ripening—indeed, they are ripe now.

Conclusion

At every point the Gospel is challenged and almost done away with, God brings Himself back to the forefront of humanity with a New Move. The wheat and the weeds are both almost fully ripe. We do not know the day or the hour of Jesus' coming, but we can clearly see that the season is drawing to its conclusion. We need another Great Awakening—a New Move—and we need to pray the house down like Simeon and Ana.

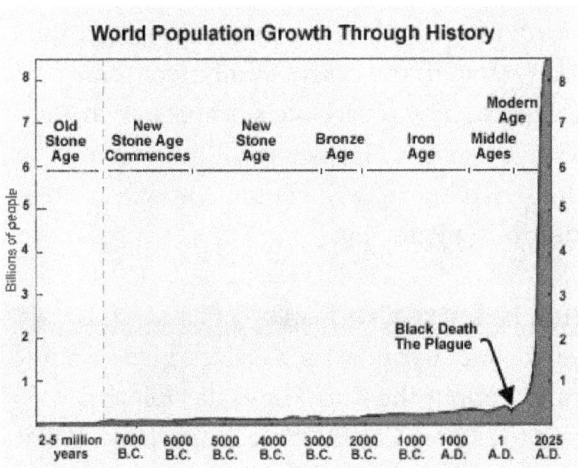

The above graph shows the growth of the human population throughout the history of mankind. Having researched many graphs from various places, they all generally hold true to the one you see here. The worldwide population does not dramatically jump up until about the 17th or 18th centuries.

I find it fascinating that the liveliest moves of the God upon the earth, (from 1500-2000) began precisely at the moment the human population worldwide begins its spectacular, meteoric rise. There have always been fringe movements of the Spirit throughout Christian history from the time of Constantine to the 1st Great Awakening. But the closer we are to the End, the more intensely the Holy Spirit is breaking onto center stage, and it is mirroring the growth of humanity. More people live today than in the rest of combined human history up to this point. God is preparing for a New Move because "He is not willing that any should perish but that all should come to repentance" (2 Peter 3:9).

PRAYING IN THESE END TIMES
I am sure that anyone who has even given a shred of thought about the End Times has felt that it seems futile to pray or much less intercede. What

are we going to pray for? That the biblical prophecies don't come to pass? The thought of many people is to not pray at all for the world because everything is already pre-determined and that's how it's going to be. We pray generally for peace, or for people we know, or for general well being in our families and churches. The world is such a scary place right now and the task of taking it on it prayer seems so daunting and insurmountable that it is easier to not do it at all.

Let me offer another perspective in light of what has been discussed in this chapter: God is not done with His Church! As long as Jesus has not come back yet, there is still war to engage in against the devil and countless souls to win for Jesus! There is still evil in the world that fights against God's people, so Psalm 141:5b instructs us, "For still my prayer is against the deeds of the wicked." Our prayers matter, and God uses them to unleash His power to curb hell's influence over the hearts and minds of the people He died to save. Heaven wants to intersect earth—but Heaven needs our prayers!

We remember that our prayers are not ***against*** people and that our intercession is ***for*** people. God loves people. Our battle is not with people, but with the devil and his demons (Ephesians 6:12). We are also commanded to love both our neighbors and our enemies (Luke 10:25-37; Matthew 5:44; 1 John 4:7-8). As we face these coming days of tribulation, persecution, and deeping evil, we remember that there is still a battle for human souls that needs our intercession. God is preparing to unleash a New Move on the earth. Pray the House Down!

10
THE WORKS OF THE LORD

Having taken a brief walk through the works of the Lord through history, let's briefly go back to the passage of the Potter and the clay in Isaiah 64. The beginning of this same passage gives us a greater context in which these words were spoken which is worthy of deeper study. In fact, the opening words of the passage are exactly what our fervent prayer is for: A New Move of God!

"Oh, that You would rend the heavens!
That You would come down!
That the mountains might shake at
Your presence—As fire burns brushwood,
as fire causes water to boil—to make Your name
known to Your adversaries, that the nations may
tremble at Your presence! When You did
awesome things for which we did not look,
You came down, the mountains shook at Your

presence. For since the beginning of the world men have not heard nor perceived by the ear, nor has the eye seen any God besides You, who acts ***for the one who waits for Him***. You meet him who rejoices and does righteousness, who remembers You in Your ways. You are indeed angry, for we have sinned—in these ways we continue; and we need to be saved." (Isaiah 64:1-5)

Look at what this is saying; that for those who wait on the Lord, ears have not heard nor eye has seen the greatness of what God wants to do. In verse one, the prophet cries out, "Oh that you would rend the heavens...!" We are to be a Church of intense seeking for this very thing: That God would tear open the heavens and come upon our churches. And for those who wait upon the Lord, we can't even conceive the great things God is going to do.

Four versus later, The prophet is repenting for sin, and it is in this context that he declares that God is the Potter and we are the clay. In his crying out for the supernatural and for the intervention of God and for the manifestation of his presence, in the midst of repenting for in, the prophet is saying, "Here we are. We are clay in your hands." The Apostle Paul uses this same passage:

"However, we speak wisdom among those who are mature, yet not the wisdom of this age, nor of the rulers of this age, who are coming to nothing. But we speak the wisdom of God in a mystery, the hidden wisdom which God ordained before the ages for our glory, which none of the rulers of this age knew; for had they known, they would not have crucified the Lord of glory. But as it is written:

'Eye has not seen, nor ear heard,
Nor have entered into the heart of man
The things which God has prepared for those who love Him.'

But God has revealed them to us through His Spirit. For the Spirit searches all things, yes, the deep things of God. For what man knows the things of a man except the spirit of the man which is in him? Even so no one knows the things of God except the Spirit of God. [12] Now we have received, not the spirit of the world, but the Spirit who is from God, that we might know the things that have been freely given to us by God." (1 Corinthians 2:6-12)

In this passage, Paul directly cites Isaiah 64, and then differentiates between divine and human wisdom. Human wisdom is not able to perceive what God is doing; only the spirit in us in communication with the Holy Spirit can understand what God is going to do in the world. To those who are spiritually mature, those who have learned to wait upon the Lord and listen to His voice, He makes known what He wants to do. For those who love Him and wait on Him, no eye has seen no ear has heard the magnitude of what He is going to do. No human being can understand this except that the Spirit of God reveal it. Psalm 25:14 says, "The secret of the Lord is for those who fear him, and then he will reveal his covenant." God is willing to give revelation, and He is looking for people who wait upon Him and fear Him to reveal His secrets.

This is one of the reasons the world around us thinks us crazy. Because in their mind and in their flesh, they cannot perceive the working of God around them. But we can. We do not follow the world's way of being because we know God is working, but for the culture around us it looks foolish.

There is a "New Move" God is getting ready to unleash on the earth, in His Church, and each one of our personal lives for which we must be prepared. This requires ears to hear, and eyes to see in the spiritual and the prophetic, and hearts to obey His voice. The Bible says in Matthew 5:8 that those who are pure in heart will see God. Matthew 7:7 says that those who seek will find.

Matthew 25:29 says that he who has more, more will be given. Jeremiah 33:3 says that if we call out to God, He will show us great and mighty things that we do not know. Isaiah 64:4 says that he who waits on the Lord will see God move in action.

When we seek, when we cry out, when we fear Him and keep our lives pure, we will have a greater revelation of who God is, what He's doing in our lives, in His Church, in our communities, and around the world along with the promise of His intimate presence.

We have a great promise that God will do great things among us, things that no ear has heard nor eye has seen nor mind has known. What God wants to do with us and what He wants to do through His Church is greater than we can fully know.

THE ARMY OF GOD
God is raising up army for a worldwide assault. This is not a physical assault; it is an assault of prayer, intercession, supernatural signs and wonders, and evangelism. For this to happen, the Church must rise up as an army. God is releasing the supernatural on His Church in new and powerful ways. God needs an army who is prepared, big, armed, and advancing because He has a greater and greater things for us to

accomplish.

Isaiah 64 also speaks of the fire of God. This is a consuming fire which, according to the passage, causes water to boil and makes His name famous among the nations. In other words, Isaiah is saying that this fire, which is the fire of His holiness and of His Holy Spirit, is what set Heaven's events in motion on the earth.

Fire is what incites movement and change. The heat of the fire water boils, burns wood, and cooks food. If it was not for the fire of God in our lives, we would be completely cold toward Him. Jesus says the same thing about the church in Laodicea. They used to be on fire and passionate for Christ Jesus, but they had cooled down to being lukewarm. And it is the lukewarm church Jesus says He will spit out of His mouth. Life in the kingdom of God is all or nothing. In God's mind, there is no such thing as a disciple of Jesus who has one foot in the world and one foot in His Kingdom. God wants to consume in us everything that does not belong to Him. He wants to light our hearts on fire with an ardent passion for His presence. We must maintain the flame of the Holy Spirit alive and burning inside of us.

It is the holiness of the Holy Spirit which is revealed in fire. But the Holy Spirit is also revealed in oil. Oil and fire go hand-in-hand. In the book of Revelation, the churches are represented by lampstands. The lamp provides light, but the oil is the fuel that maintains the frame. The prophecy of Isaiah 64 speaks of this fire reviving and saving God's people to take His name to the nations.

Without the oil and the fire of the Holy Spirit, nothing will happen. It is the Holy Spirit who does the work, not us. In order for God to use us, we must be open to what he wants to give us and however He wishes to use us.

II
POTS OF OIL

"A certain woman of the wives of the sons of the prophets cried out to Elisha, saying, 'Your servant my husband is dead, and you know that your servant feared the LORD. And the creditor is coming to take my two sons to be his slaves.' So Elisha said to her, 'What shall I do for you? Tell me, what do you have in the house?' And she said, 'Your maidservant has nothing in the house but a jar of oil.'

Then he said, 'Go, borrow vessels from everywhere, from all your neighbors—empty vessels; do not gather just a few. And when you have come in, you shall shut the door behind you and your sons; then pour it into all those vessels, and set aside the full ones.'

So she went from him and shut the door behind her and her sons, who brought the vessels to her;

and she poured it out. Now it came to pass, when the vessels were full, that she said to her son, "Bring me another vessel."

And he said to her, 'There is not another vessel.' So the oil ceased. [7] Then she came and told the man of God. And he said, 'Go, sell the oil and pay your debt; and you and your sons live on the rest.'" (2 Kings 4:1-7)

This woman didn't have hope in the world. She didn't have anything more than a flask of oil. She's at the point of losing everything, including her children, who are more than just beloved family members; they were also her security in her old age. This is the state of our world today. Satan has people enslaved because they are dead in sin. Through this indebted slavery he is stealing our present and our future.

This woman found the answer: she went to the man of God, and God did a miracle. The miracle of provision for this woman was not only in the miraculous flow of oil, it was also in the clay jars. She did not borrow a few small jars. She got big ones able to hold lots of oil. This was the solution to her dilemma.

God is making us bigger. God is forming us so that we can hold more oil of His presence and anointing.

There is a world full of people who are lost and who need an answer for their lives. The answer is clay pots filled with oil—*and we are those clay pots!* We are the clay in the hands of the Potter. God is enlarging us because He wants to fill us with His presence, His glory, His Spirit and His supernatural power as never before because our lives are the answer to the world around us. Our lives are the answer for our families and our nation, but God needs to prepare us, and God does not want "just a few."

This calling is not only for pastors and leaders, but for every follower of Jesus Christ. Not a few people, many! Jesus needs people who are big and filled with the Holy Spirit. But we must allow ourselves to be formed by God into something greater that He can use. We are in a time of active waiting, but it is incumbent upon all of us to allow ourselves to be on the Potter's wheel and let Him do to us and in us according to His will so we can fulfill His purposes.

There's no time for sin. There's no time for contentious divisions, gossip, or lies. There's no time to divide our love between God and our sinful desires. It's time to seek God, to know His heart, to give ourselves fully to His process in our lives. Let yourself be formed by the Potter! Right there where you are right now, I want you to make this prayer:

Lord my God, I come to you expecting the fulfillment of your work in me, knowing that He who began to work in me will be faithful to finish it. I give myself completely up to you. I ask that you put me on your potter's wheel to make me exactly how you want me to be. Take out of me any impurity. Do what you need to do with me so that I may be used to maximize your Kingdom here on earth. Give me strength and perseverance to wait during your process. I give to my expectations, and with simplicity and humility I give Myself to your purposes. In the name of Jesus Christ. Amen.

12
PERSONAL PREPARATION

In preparation for what God has for us we need to do many things. The enlargement God is working in us comes in different forms. Over the next pages I want to challenge how we respond to the Lord and His work in our lives. There are three areas we will briefly discuss: repentance, serving, and worship. Each of these areas is a tremendous way in which God enlarges our lives. Each of us must choose to live in a way that pleases God. In other words, there is a price to pay to see the greatness of God revealed in our lives, and the price requires the removal sin from our lives.

I pray that God gives to each of us the gift of repentance. Repentance is more than simply saying I'm sorry; it is a total life change. However, this is not a life change that we can make on our own. Sin is too strong for our feeble human flesh.

God needs to help us even to have genuine repentance—this is why I say it is a "gift of repentance." This is the kind of repentance that breaks our hearts in such a way that God can put His hand into the center of our being and take out the ugliness of sin that resides there. Remember the same power that raised Christ from the dead lives in us; therefore, we can expect that with a profound and healing repentance, we can live the same supernatural life that Jesus did and a life completely free from sin as Jesus did.

Sin cannot be taken lightly. If we have a light view of sin, we will have a light view of God's amazing grace. If we have a light view of God's grace, then sin is no longer a big deal and we will constantly go back into it. Read what 2 Corinthians 7:10-11 says regarding this gift of repentance:

"For godly sorrow produces repentance leading to salvation, not to be regretted; but the sorrow of the world produces death. For observe this very thing, that you sorrowed in a godly manner: What diligence it produced in you, what clearing of yourselves, what indignation, what fear, what vehement desire, what zeal, what vindication! In all things you proved yourselves to be clear in this matter."

This passage tells us what happens in a person

when there is a supernatural, profound, and healing repentance. Such repentance produces: 1) diligence, 2) clearing of yourselves, 3) indignation, 4) fear, 5) vehement desire, 6) zeal, and 7) vindication. The seven concepts are the result of what a deep and transformative repentance produces in our lives.

Diligence

True repentance will produce diligence in our lives. The Greek word translated here for diligence also means fervor and seriousness. As the Holy Spirit reveals our sin and the actual condition of our hearts, we become very fervent and diligent in our desire to get our lives right with Jesus. We don't allow ourselves to play around with sin anymore. As Philippians 2:12 says, we "tend to [work out] our salvation." We do this by stripping every trace of sin from our lives so our condition before God is not sullied.

If you were to put on white clothing, whatever mark or spot is on there will become visible in contrast to the white material. I am sure that you, as well as I, have put on something white before, and when inevitably we spilled food on the shirt, we react with some consternation and diligence to get the spot out before it sets into a stain because nobody likes looking dirty! But when we put on clothing of darker color or pattern clothing, the stain is not as readily visible and sometimes the urgency is not the same because the clothing can hide the stain—sometimes we may not even notice.

When our lives are dirtied up with sin, other sins might conceal it. A little sin doesn't seem to be a big deal when there are other huge, glaring, and obvious sins that eclipse it; it may even look like it belongs there! But if our lives are pure as God desires them to be, if we are dressed in the white of righteousness and salvation (see Isaiah 61:10), then even the smallest spot will provoke fervor in us to keep clean. When we truly walk in the purity of God, we notice every sin, and with diligence and seriousness and fervor we work to keep ourselves clean before Him. True repentance will produce purity and diligence to keep us clean.

CLEARING OF YOURSELVES

With the gift of repentance, along with diligence, will come the desire to exonerate our name before God. When Paul says here "clearing of yourselves" the Greek term used is that of a legal defense before a judge. This is not self-justification or a frivolous explanation of our sins. This is coming before the throne of God asking for his mercy. We do not deserve to receive such clemency from the great Judge, but God gives it because of His great love that He showed us in the death and resurrection of His Son, Jesus Christ while we were still sinners. Jesus lived the life we should have lived, and died the death we should have died so that through Him we could be right with God. When we are before God, Jesus advocates for us. He is our advocate whose defense exonerates us of our guilt and expunges our record before God. 1 John 2:1-3 says,

"My little children, these things I write to you, so that you may not sin. And if anyone sins, we have an Advocate with the Father, Jesus Christ the righteous. And He Himself is the propitiation for our sins, and not for ours only but also for the whole world."

Take note that the end of this passage speaks of diligence, not only the forgiveness from sins. Our judge and advocate, Jesus, forgives us, but we must be diligent in knowing him and keeping his commandments. Such is the effect of the true gift of repentance.

INDIGNATION

True repentance will produce in us righteous indignation towards sin. If sin is not repugnant to us, then there still exists some love or tolerance of it in our lives. Sin should do much more than just break our hearts; it should cause righteous anger in us because it contaminated us before the holiness of God, and it works to destroy us and the people around us.

When Jesus raised Lazarus from the dead in John 11, the Bible says that "a deep anger welled up within Him," (NLT) when He came to Lazarus's tomb. The Greek word used in this passage is one that is used for a horse that snorts when it is angry—furious and ready to charge. Why was Jesus angry if He knew He was going to raise Lazarus from the dead? It could be for the lack of faith in the people around. But Jesus already had told His disciples that it would be through this miracle they would believe in Him.

I believe the cause of such anger in Jesus was because of death itself. Sin brings death. When Jesus arrived at Lazarus' tomb, He became angry because He knew that such is the destiny of all who sin. But God so loved the world that He gave His only Son that whoever believes in Him would not die but have eternal life. God hates all sin, not just some sins. All sin is repugnant to Him, and true, profound repentance should cause us the same anger toward what sin does to people

FEAR
True repentance will produce in us the fear of God. Such repentance gives honor and respect to God. We will honor the Lord so much that we will

be afraid to violate His holiness, and we will tremble at the thought that our actions would grieve the Holy Spirit who lives in us. Sinning will not longer be easy or natural for us. If sin is not a fearful thing for us, then the divine revelation of the gravity of sin and the splendor of the holiness of God need to become more real to us. If we can easily sin, we lack the fear of God.

The fear of the Lord will give much greater revelation and understanding of God. Psalm 25:14 says, "The Lord is a friend to those who fear Him; and to them He will reveal His covenant." God will trust greater revelation to those who have respect for Him, and He will consider them His close, personal friends. Psalm 66:18 also says, "If I had not confessed my sin from my heart, the Lord would not have heard me." In other words, those who fear the Lord will be taught by him as a close friend, but God will not even listen to those do not confess and deal with sin.

Vehement Desire

The gift of true and profound repentance will produce in us an intense desire, a passion and love for God that we did not know before. When Jesus had dinner with a certain Pharisee and a sinful woman came and spilled her tears over His feet, several the house rebuked her, but Jesus forgave her. And in Luke 7:47, Jesus spoke to the situation saying, "Therefore I say to you, her sins, which are many, are forgiven, , For she loved much. But to whom little is forgiven, the same loves little." If the flame of our love is going out, then there is sin in our hearts that needs to be dealt with.

When we treat sin is something light, then our repentance will be likewise, superficial. When repentance is superficial, our love will be the same because we will not perceive the forgiveness and the love of God has something great. When we diminish the ugliness of sin, we will never be able to truly understand how great God's grace is toward us. But where sin abounds, God's grace abounds much more (Romans 5:20). The grace of God cannot abound where there is no recognition and repentance from the abundance of sin in our own hearts. And the Holy Spirit reveals the condition of our hearts and God forgives us of that same condition. How could our love not grow for him and how could we not have more passion for his presence?

ZEAL

True and deep repentance will produce zeal and cause us see God's presence move and grow and pour out of our lives and our churches. God's presence will not move in a life or a church where sin is persistent. There are a few reasons for this: 1) God wants to use vessels that are clean as He is clean; 2) God responds in a different way to those who passionately desire Him.

When a man falls in love with a woman and begins to try and win her heart, he doesn't do it half-heartedly. He will use all his zeal and passion to win the love of his life. Besides that, what woman would respond to a man who shows only a little bit of interest in her? In the same way, why would God respond with His wonderful presence to someone who barely recognizes He is there? In Psalm 69:9 says, "Zeal for your house has consumed me."

The person who lives in true and deep repentance will also have zeal for the presence of God, and subsequently, will see what the heart most desires. Matthew 5:8 says, "Blessed are the pure in heart, for they will see God." This does not mean only someday we're going to see God in Heaven, but we're going to see Him in new ways and more profound ways in our lives and in our Churches. Our spiritual eyes will be opened to draw even closer to Him and see Him with more clarity. Just as intimate friendship with God and revelation of God are for those who fear Him, those who keep themselves pure and maintain the flame of their love and passion for the presence of God will see Him be enlarged in their lives. Psalm 24:3-4 says,

"Who may ascend into the hill of the LORD? Or who may stand in His holy place? He who has clean hands and a pure heart, who has not lifted up his soul to an idol, nor sworn deceitfully."

This kind of zeal and passion and purity is catalytic for the presence of God.

Profound and genuine repentance from our sins and a hatred for the same sins will not only cause zeal for God, but will attract His presence, His joy, His anointing, and His miracles signs and wonders. When there is hatred towards sin and a passion toward God, the anointing of the Holy Spirit will become greater and greater in our lives. If there is not supernatural power flowing through our lives, or we have become apathetic towards the presence of God; if we are stagnant in our walk with God and we feel we cannot advance, if we are on the point of throwing in the towel with God, we need to ask the Holy Spirit to reveal to us the areas of our lives where persistent sin is weighing us down. Sin is a passion-killer. Sin grieves the Holy Spirit. Sin destroys the disciples of Jesus Christ. Sin will cause us to fall away from God. We must repent of our sins and receive all the life and goodness that God has for us. One evangelist is quoted as saying:

"I know many Christians, even sinners, who say

they cannot be perfect, and it is useless to even try. We know who they are. They are not healing the sick nor casting out demons. Sin is the entry point of the devil in your life. You can allow it to persist if you want, but it will rob you of your power!"

VINDICATION

True and genuine repentance will give us vindication from our sins. At the end of his discourse over repentance to the Corinthian's, Paul says, "You have shown yourselves to be clean in this issue [of sin and repentance]." When we repent genuinely with a supernatural gift of repentance, there is forgiveness and freedom. 1 John 1:9, "If we confess our sins, He is faithful and just to forgive us our sins and to cleanse us from all unrighteousness." And Psalm 118:5 says, "I called on the LORD in distress;
The LORD answered me and set me in a broad place."

Before we were dirty, ashamed, guilty, and condemned, but repentance changed the whole situation. Now we are exonerated of our sins and free!

13
SERVICE AND WORSHIP

Jesus Christ did not save us only so that we could go to Heaven someday but that we would become the "measure of the stature of the fullness of Christ Jesus" (Ephesians 4:13). In order to cultivate a life that is being formed by the hands of the Potter to the image of Christ Jesus, we must surrender ourselves completely to Him. Romans 12:1 says our lives are given to the Lord through being a living sacrifice. The sacrifice of our lives is reflected in living out a life of worship and obedience to the Lord. This is the central concept of being a living sacrifice to the Lord. Our sacrifice to the Lord is more that are songs of worship, it is found in how we follow the Lord, how we give ourselves to Him, how we obey Him, and how we love and serve others.

SERVICE IS WORSHIP

Life of service to God is living a life of worship. In the Garden of Eden, there was no specified worship. There were no sacrifices because there was no need for them. We know of nothing that could be thought of as "worship" as we perceive it in our minds today. But what God did give Adam were two things: 1) His image and 2) a mandate.

As Adam was made in the image of God, he was uniquely prepared to participate with God as His representative and as His co-laborer. What distinguished Adam from the rest of creation was that God breathed in him the "breath of life" to make him a living being. In other words, Adam was given the same spirit to bring about the purposes of God for which he was created. There is nothing else in all of creation that can do the things the human being was made to do. And our purpose, as the image of God, is to do the same things God would do; we were made to fully participate alongside him in his creation.

Along with God's image, God gave Adam a mandate which we find in Genesis 1:28; 2:15:

"Then God blessed them, and God said to them, "Be fruitful and multiply; fill the earth and subdue it; have dominion over the fish of the sea, over the birds of the air, and over every living thing that moves on the earth…Then the Lord God took the man and put him in the garden of Eden to tend and keep it."

Adam was to participate with God stewarding the garden. He was to work, take care of, protect, develop, discover, and serve the garden in the same way God Himself would have done it. The Hebrew word for "serve" used in other places in the Bible is the priestly work in the temple of God. Adam was to be a type of priest in the Garden, and Adam's worship to God was in his service, his work, his protection, and development of the garden. God was to be exalted when His co-laborer did the same things He Himself would have done.

We each have a garden God has given to us. This garden is everything we are, everything we have, and every person God has placed in our lives. Our gardens are our lives. Our service is our worship to God. When we love and serve people who come into the sphere of the garden God has given us, we are both serving and worshiping. The way we speak, the way we take care of ourselves, and the way we take care of others are all part of protecting and making our garden flourish. But when we live in anger and unforgiveness, in sin, selfishness, pride, and destructive patterns, it's like swinging a machete over all the beautiful flowers

God has planted in our garden. We are destroying our garden and doing the opposite of what God would do. Using our lives to serve and love others is living as a sacrifice of worship to God.

Service also has to do with our churches. Part of our gardens is the family of believers in which God has placed us. I want to challenge you if you are not serving any part of the church, it's time to allow God to enlarge your life. One way to do this is by serving your church family to help it grow and flourish. We are better and we are stronger when all of us participate! Let your service that you give to the Lord be part of your worship as well.

Worship and Surrender

As part of our God given mandate to participate in His same works, the Lord challenged me regarding how I live as a person and how we live as a church. I remember one day, a while ago, I was listening to a woman give a prophecy and she said, "My [God's] Church is not as powerful as it should be. I [God] have given you salvation, My Holy Spirit, power to heal the sick, power to do miracles, and you are not doing them." When I heard this I felt very convicted. Right there I knelt down and I said to the Lord, "Teach me. Speak to me. What do you want to do? How do you want to do it? I need your instruction." In that moment the

Holy Spirit spoke to me and lead me to Matthew 26. The story we are going to read is found in all four Gospels of Matthew, Mark, Luke, and John and every time the story is told, different aspects come out in each book. The following is a compilation of the four different biblical versions:

"Meanwhile, Jesus was in Bethany at the home of Simon, a man who had previously had leprosy. While he was eating, a woman came in with a beautiful alabaster jar of expensive perfume made from essence of nard, and poured it over his head, and she anointed Jesus' feet with it, wiping his feet with her hair. The house was filled with the fragrance. When the Pharisee who had invited him saw this, he said to himself, "If this man were a prophet, he would know what kind of woman is touching him. She's a sinner!"

Then Jesus answered his thoughts. "Simon," he said to the Pharisee, "I have something to say to you." "Go ahead, Teacher," Simon replied.

Then Jesus told him this story: "A man loaned money to two people—500 pieces of silver to one and 50 pieces to the other. But neither of them could repay him, so he kindly forgave them both, canceling their debts. Who do you suppose loved him more after that?"

Simon answered, "I suppose the one for whom he canceled the larger debt." "That's right," Jesus said. Then he turned to the woman and said to Simon, "Look at this woman kneeling here. When I entered your home, you didn't offer me water to wash the dust from my feet, but she has washed them with her tears and wiped them with her hair. You didn't greet me with a kiss, but from the time I first came in, she has not stopped kissing my feet. You neglected the courtesy of olive oil to anoint my head, but she has anointed my feet with rare perfume."

"I tell you, her sins—and they are many—have been forgiven, so she has shown me much love. But a person who is forgiven little shows only little love." Then Jesus said to the woman, "Your sins are forgiven." Some of those at the table were indignant. "Why waste such expensive perfume?" they asked. "It could have been sold for a year's wages and the money given to the poor!" So they scolded her harshly. But Jesus replied, "Leave her alone. Why criticize her for doing such a good thing to me? You will always have the poor among you, and you can help them whenever you want to. But you will not always have me. She has done what she could and has anointed my body for burial ahead of time. [9] I tell you the truth, wherever the Good News is preached throughout the world, this woman's deed will be remembered and discussed." (NLT)

This woman had a treasure in an alabaster jar. It was a very costly perfume that was valued at about a years salary, let's put it at about $60,000. If I had something in my house that was worth that much, I think I would also count it among my treasures! I would have it stored away and protected. Who knows how long she had held onto this perfume, maybe it was for many years.

When my wife and I were first married, somebody gave us a complete set of Brazilian porcelain plates for eight people with hand-painted flowers on them. They are very beautiful and for years we did not use them. We never found an occasion special enough to take them out and use such fine dishes. For all this time, there were those plates sitting there very pretty stored in boxes in the garage. Sometime later we realized we were depriving ourselves of using these plates. We decided that we would either give them away, or we would eventually break all of them with use, but we had to do something with them! We made the decision to use them. They were made for that, weren't they? And now they sit in our cabinets being used with a degree of frequency.

I like backpacking in the woods. One of the greatest things about backpacking is that you get to carry a knife! I love camping knives. Over the years I have bought a few knives mostly in the

$20-$30 range. A few years ago, a friend of mine who shares the camping knife affinity with me, give me a very fine knife that cost about $250. I probably never would have spent so much on a camping knife, but I was extremely grateful! For quite some time I kept using my cheap knives so I wouldn't dirty or scratch up the nice knife or dull the blade. After a few years, I realized how ridiculous this was. Why have it if I'm never going to use it? Why deny myself the pleasure of being able to use something of such a good quality while I continue to use something of a much inferior quality? Now I use it every chance I get. Yes, it's a bit scratched, a bit dirty, a little less sharp than it used to be, but I so enjoy using it!

This sinful woman had something of much greater value, much more than my plates and knives! If you possessed a perfume that cost $60,000, you're not going to break the jar and pour it all out all at once on one person. You would use only a few drops at a time so that it would last you years because it is such a costly treasure. But she took the entirety of her treasure, and she used it on Jesus.

The reality is that Jesus has given something very costly to each one of us. He's given us salvation. He has given us the power of his Holy Spirit. God has equipped and calibrated his Church to participate in advancing in His Kingdom by preaching with power, sharing the Gospel, putting our hands up on the sick and seeing them healed, doing miracles, and casting out demons. This is not only for pastors who are those who consider themselves "super spiritual." This is available for every person who believes in Jesus Christ. If God has never used you to work a miracle, heal a sick person, or has used any of the other gifts of the Holy Spirit through you, why? We have everything in Jesus. Perhaps your life is not properly calibrated to spiritual issues, but this is part of the enlargement God wants to work in your life and in our churches. He wants to use us in the supernatural. It's time to allow God to form us shape us into a form so that He can begin to use us at a different level in our church.

Just as this woman had her treasures stored up in her house for years, we have the treasure of our salvation and the power of the Holy Spirit in us. Many times this stays bottled up just to be admired but without usage to its full potential.

As human beings, we have a tendency to live in fear of losing what we have, or we live in fear that we are unworthy. We have the fear of taking out and using the treasure given to us. Maybe somebody might think that would cost too much or that God would require a sacrifice that's too great for us to give—but He does want the sacrifice of our lives. Yet, if we have the treasure of salvation, I ask you if this is truly the treasure you have in your heart. Jesus said that where your treasure is your heart will be. Maybe your treasure is your child. Maybe your treasure is your comfortability. It's easier to live in Jesus without breaking the alabaster jar and spending what's inside. Then why have it? Maybe your treasure is your pride of always being right in everything. Or maybe it is the fear that if God breaks you open and uses your life to its full capacity, it would be a disaster. If that's where you live, that's where your heart is—loving God in word but staying in your own comfort zone. Jesus did not save us so that we could have an easy and comfortable Christianity. He saved us to advance his Kingdom in the power of His Spirit and to enjoy an intimate relationship with Him. This is the very same Jesus who wants the unique treasure of your life. He wants to adjust us, reform us to become bigger and more useful for His purposes.

This woman made a decision: she took her most costly treasure and brought it to Jesus. She used it on His head and His feet. She took the alabaster jar and did not just open it, she broke it open. That is not how you use costly perfume, but that's what she did to anoint Jesus.

The anointing was the preparation for the next thing Jesus was going to do. Jesus himself said that this was in preparation for His death, which was the next step in God's plan of salvation for us. We cry out to Jesus for His anointing, which is a worthy prayer. But we never think of us anointing Jesus. This woman prepared Jesus for the next step in His ministry which was the fulfillment of our salvation. But when we pour out our anointing, our worship over Jesus is the preparation for the next thing He is going to do in our church and in our personal lives.

It is the worship of a heart that has been broken which makes room for the New Move of God in his or her life. We have a treasure inside of us, and when we begin to anoint Jesus with the same treasure He has given to us, this is when we honor Him with our worship, and we give Him the greatest welcome in our worship. Such a preparation and such worship require brokenness in our lives. If we do not allow ourselves to be broken before the Lord, the treasure in our hearts will never be fully used or reach its maximum potential. It is the same as not using the plates or the knives, I have them, but they don't do anything if they're not used.

Worship in the Old Testament has everything to do sacrifice. Sacrifice is something you give at great cost to yourself. It is giving the best of one's self. Many times when the people of God lived a life of pleasing worship to God through their obedience and humility, the Bible says that such worship "came up before the Lord has a *fragrant* offering." Romans 12:1 says that we offer ourselves as living sacrifices to the Lord. When we live in the way that pleases him, our whole life which we offer in complete surrender, is a fragrant offering to Him.

In the same way, when the woman broke the alabaster jar, the Bible says it fragrance filled the house. When we decide to live a life of service and worship to the Lord, the fragrance of our lives will fill all the world around us. Our families, our friends, our work associates will all see God's beauty in our lives. We will also experience the fragrance of His presence, His voice, and in intimate relationship with Him. His life and power will flow from the life of humility and brokenness lived before Jesus in worship and service. And this way we are not hiding what God gave us, but we are releasing all the beauty and effectiveness that the alabaster jars of our lives has because the Holy Spirit lives in us.

What I desire in my personal life, as well is in the Church of Jesus Christ, more than any other thing is the fragrance of the Presence of God and the fragrance of our lives of worship. Let yourself be broken and used by the Lord. The broken life is the life that God can most use.

At the end of the story, Jesus said that wherever this Gospel is heard, this woman will be honored. With such brokenness, with such worship, with such an anointing, and with such fearless love, she was honored by Jesus. In this moment, Jesus links together love, brokenness, and the anointing poured out upon Himself with the spreading of the Gospel around the world. Just think about it. The Gospel has reached your town 2000 years afterward, and we're still telling the story! Now, everything we do in the Church is for the purpose of reaching people for Jesus. But He just wants to bring more people to know Him, many more than those who have been reached up to this point.

Our worship has something to do with this, just as this woman anointed Jesus for the next thing Jesus was going to do. Perhaps in our worship we are anointing Jesus as well. He's waiting to do more in His people and it is incumbent upon us to worship Him, to anoint Him, and give Him permission to work. Jesus will honor this. Let's anoint Jesus in preparation for the "New Move" He is getting ready to unleash around the world. Pray the house down!

About the Author

Kyle W. Bauer has a rich ministry history spanning nearly two decades. Throughout his career, he's served as a children's pastor, a church planter, a missionary in Mexico, and a professor of ministry and history at the King's University and at La Facultad de Teología. His current ministry assignment is serving as the senior pastor at Pathway, in Northridge, CA. Kyle holds a Bachelor's Degree in Theological Studies and a Master's Degree in Divinity, both from The King's University. He and his wife, Teresa, were married in 2003 and have four children—three boys, and one girl.

For more information or to contact Kyle, you can visit his site www.kwbauer.com

His books are available in English and Spanish at www.amazon.com

www.ingramcontent.com/pod-product-compliance
Lightning Source LLC
Chambersburg PA
CBHW031403040426
42444CB00005B/401